THE JOY OF ANXIETY

TRANSFORMING YOUR WORRY TO WONDER IN THE SECOND HALF OF LIFE

ALSO BY SUE LEGACY

The Joy Of Nada

THE JOY OF ANXIETY

TRANSFORMING YOUR WORRY TO WONDER
IN THE SECOND HALF OF LIFE

SUE LEGACY

Copyright © 2015 by Sue Genaro Legacy

EMAIL: info@thejoyofanxiety.com

WEBSITE: www.thejoyofanxiety.com.

ISBN-13: 978-1506197876   ISBN-10: 1506197876

Library of Congress Control Number: 2015914523

CreateSpace Independent Publishing Platform, N. Charleston, SC

This book is dedicated to anyone who has ever suffered from anxiety.

Special Offer

Please see the back of this book for a special offer in appreciation of your taking the time to read it.

CONTENTS

INTRODUCTION

"Wonder is the beginning of wisdom."— Socrates

Worries and fears are with us from childhood until death. They are part of the human experience we all share while on this earth, no matter our age, nor any amount of wisdom we amass. This mature realization did not hit me until I reached the second stage of life. My hope had been that the anxiety of my youth would morph into calmness and peace of mind, and that wisdom would magically appear to guide me into old age.

Yet when I turned fifty, I discovered a new reality – that we will always have anxieties, worries and fears; they will just be different from the first half of life. Our youthful self-consciousness may wane and fears of making the wrong decision may no longer immobilize us. Though now we have end of life, financial stability and the meaning of our life worries.

Because my childhood insecurities had been so prominent in my life, I spent way too much time wishing serenity would mystically appear when I most needed it — overwhelmed with worry and doubt. I didn't consider how my anxiety could bring me unexpected benefits. I certainly never imagined that I could learn how to find joy from my worries.

However, after twenty-three years as a social worker and psychotherapist who helps others with their problems, I have found that when we pay attention to our thoughts and discover the hidden meaning of our anxieties, we can see those worries as gifts - gifts in the form of self-knowledge and wisdom, which will allow us to discover the *joy* that lies within us.

What if you didn't have to *hope* for your anxiety to disappear and for comfort to magically appear? What if you could experience joy by exploring what *causes* your worries? What if you could find a new appreciation, even gratitude for a past regret that once only seemed to anger and depress you? And what if instead of viewing anxiety as a barrier to happiness and something to avoid, you could see it as a gift?

I've discovered that in order to change the way we view anxiety, we first need to acknowledge and accept that worries are a part of our humanity. Acknowledge the reality that unexamined anxiety can be insidious.

Once we accept that as truth, we can begin the process investigating our fears and see them simply as an evil twin to unexpected joy. I want to help you uncover these gifts.

Come along on a journey to accept how anxiety is part of the human experience, and discover how it can be both a scary roommate **and** a welcomed friend in our lives. Through this guide you can discover how the joy of anxiety can be the joy of being human.

Sue Legacy

THE JOY OF ANXIETY

1

THE FUTURE IS NOW

"Anxiety, the illness of our time, comes primarily from our inability to dwell in the present moment."

ThichNhatHanh, *The Heart of the Buddha's Teaching: Transforming Suffering into Peace, Joy, and Liberation*

Anxiety sucks. It just does.

Anxiety is a worry, nervousness, or fear about an event with an uncertain outcome. An uncertain outcome? If you have ever been a worrier, wouldn't that pertain to just about *everything* in life? Couldn't one obsess about the responsibilities of today, tomorrow, and even the past? All those things we did we wish we hadn't.

All those things that happened to us or by us that we either regret, feel hurt by, shamed about, or worse, have never mentioned because to mention them would bring them to life. And if we brought them to our consciousness and spoke or wrote our truths, someone might disagree or dislike us. They might think we are stupid, dumb, incompetent, imperfect, or worse, human.

So, we worry.

Being a therapist, I know that we worry about what others think of us if we expose our anxieties. We know that no one is perfect, but we don't always like to reveal our humanity.

My own anxiety has been the pest that won't die despite lots of various and sundry pest control efforts. I have tried to exterminate it for years.

I have decided that annihilation is too extreme. Besides, I always had the fear that if I was able to totally rid myself of any anxiety, it might come back with a vengeance—like a plague that had to be exorcised by a priest who might not be skilled in anxiety exorcisms.

Of course that brought up more worry, and that worry led me to the theoretical discovery, which I named Sue Legacy's Principle of Anxiety, which is: anxiety sucks!

This well-known principle of anxiety can be true whether you are in the first stage of life, the years of birth to forty-nine, or in the second half of life, age fifty and above. It can be the unwelcome crasher at parties, special events and celebrations. It arrives early and stays late. Anxiety can find us alone or in a crowd.

Once it discovers us, it isn't long before feeling unworthy and inadequate becomes more common than feeling worthwhile. Before we know it, negative thoughts can rule our mind. We can doubt any decision we make, if we can make one at all.

Anxiety has moved in, like an unwanted roommate.

For some people, however, anxiety is quiet and not as noticeable. It can knock and politely ask if you have room. You may even welcome it, believing that it has your best interests at heart. Like when your concern of becoming ill from germs found on doorknobs or through shaking hands tells you that it is okay to wash your hands over and over—it is only about being clean and staying healthy. Or when your need to keep your drawers neat and organized a certain way. Or else.

And the "or else" is that anxiety and negative thoughts about yourself will creep into your space and create the havoc you are trying so diligently to prevent. Keeping things around you organized, ensuring that the house is clean and spotless before you can get anything else accomplished, and making sure, or working very hard at making sure everything is perfect, is the goal. As long as you can do that, any anxiety or worry about your own imperfections can be kept at bay.

Whether your anxiety is quiet or loud, there is a difference between anxieties in the first part of our lives versus the second half. In the first half there are so many life issues to ponder over which we have so much doubt, worry and angst.

As youngsters we are afraid of the first day of school, even if we are excited about it at the same time. As teenagers we worry about being accepted by our peers. We might have anxiety about spending the night at a friend's house for the first time, or learning to play a musical instrument, or a new sport.

We worry about getting into college and how to pay for it, what to study for future financial stability, and how will we get our first job. We wonder who will be our first love and whether it will be everlasting. We may want children and wonder what to do if we are unable to bear them. We worry about how to support them, and how to support ourselves.

Whew! The first half of life is hard.

How do our life anxieties differ now? The second stage of life is still filled with fears about the future. You may hate what you do for a living and fear that you will never be able to quit because you want your money to outlive you, not the other way around. You may love what you do for a living, yet worry that some impairment may keep you from having the option to do what you love. You may have a mental bucket list that includes travel to all seven continents by the time you are seventy, but fear good health may not comply. Or you fulfilled your list and you think, now what?

Maybe you have accomplished all but one of the items on your bucket list and are afraid to complete that last one because if you have no more bucket list, would that mean it's time to kick the bucket?

During this stage of our lives, we worry about how long we have to live. Will we outlive our spouse; we pray not our kids, but what about our pets? When we go who will take care of them? We watch our parents age, become ill and need twenty-four-hour-a-day care. What if Mom goes before Dad? How will he survive without our help? Do we have the means to help him? Our parents are aging and dying; we are aging and dying. Who will take care of us when we no longer can?

We used to be told that retirement was an event that would just happen. Now we realize that for some of us it is more of a dream and an ideal which we may not experience. We hear Suze Orman tell us that if we continue to pay or save for our children's college, and unless we deposit a certain amount of money into a savings account, we may never be able to retire. We worry that we may never have enough income to stop worrying about it.

My good friend Mary's parents are now in their early nineties and in good health. Her father retired from his accounting business at the age of fifty-nine. He was certain he would not live beyond ten or twenty more years. Now, at ninety-one, he says he would never have retired if he had known he would live this long. His concern is living beyond his financial means.

However, I want to challenge your beliefs about aging and any time you have left on earth and show you how you can transform your worries into wonder, even joy. Despite all that we have to lose sleep over, much graver things than in the first half, we can learn to dismiss more of the first half of life insecurities and reduce the worries of the now.

Firstly, we must recognize that the uncertainties and concerns of the second half will happen. It is no longer, *What if my spouse dies before me?* Instead, unless you die together, one of you will outlive the other. So, if we know that the worries that we fear *will* happen, we need to find peace with our mortality, the inevitable course of events that we now face. We must find ways to live comfortably and joyfully *with* the anxieties that life over fifty can bring.

Secondly, if we continue to have first half of life worries and insecurities, we may need to ask ourselves what our anxiety is trying to tell us. Maybe it is a nudge to explore what might be going on within us on a deeper level that keeps those worries and fears close by; maybe there are past resentments or traumas that have not yet been resolved.

Looking back I realize my passion of helping others with their anxieties, worries and fears began with my *own* anxieties, worries and fears as a child. I was a shy third daughter from an Italian-American family whose parents had expected a son their third try but got me instead. A son means you can carry on the father's name for a future legacy. A daughter is unable to do that, so my position in the family as the third daughter was fluff, redundant, as in "been there, done that." I felt unnecessary and without purpose to my family.

On top of that I had asthma as a child, which made it hard to breathe, which made me anxious, and only made my breathing worse. The physical terror of having difficulty taking a breath increased my belief that I couldn't handle life.

Despite the genetic component of asthma and my grandfather dying from its complications, it was largely considered psychosomatic, or a physical condition caused by mental and emotional stress. My anxieties and thoughts of low self-worth were my constant shadows.

By the time I became a full-fledged social worker in 1991, well into my thirties, anxiety had become an ever-present part of my life; that unwanted roommate had morphed into a familiar companion. I fought the urge to let it become a best friend by seeking help for myself as I learned ways to help my clients.

My career began as a medical social worker at a large hospital in Atlanta, Georgia, until a position became available in a psychiatric hospital. After that I was hooked on treating depression, anxiety and other mental illness. I was fascinated with finding out what brought someone to the hospital by delving into their background to see the impact abuse, loss, neglect or trauma had on them as I learned how to help them. After working with clients of different ages, I settled on working with the adult population, clients age eighteen to fifty-five and their families.

Until one day in 1997.

I was offered a position to facilitate group counseling to adults who were over fifty-five, admitted to a local hospital for depression, anxiety, and life transition issues. I was in my forties at the time. I had never intended to work with the older adult population; after all they were *older* adults, older than me and *old*.

I may have had worries, fears and trepidations, yet I was still too young to give the second half of life much thought. But when the opportunity arose and there wasn't a position available for me in the adult wing of the hospital, it sounded like an interesting short-term job.

One morning, before I facilitated a depression and anxiety management group, a seventy-two-year-old woman remarked about my brown and black geometric patterned dress. My recollection of that dress was that the cut, neckline and belted waist were flattering. Yet, Dorothy had a different view.

"That dress makes you look fifty. It is not becoming to your youthful ways," she said.

Dorothy was one of the more vocal members of the group who felt fine voicing her opinion in a direct way. I remember being taken aback at first, even a bit hurt, and took it personally. Of course, it was personal — but her brashness was appealing. She had a boldness that younger adults do not necessarily have. Her openness, honesty, and assertive style drew me in. She and other members of the group seemed to exude wisdom despite their difficulty managing some of the changes in their lives.

I felt compelled to learn more about that age group. That day cemented my desire to continue to work with older adults so we could learn from each other how to manage any future paths we were to travel.

I never wore that dress again. I didn't want to look like that dowdy old lady Dorothy said I was. Instead of an honest self-evaluation of how I thought I looked and how much I liked that dress, I gave in to my anxiety over how somehow else thought I looked and stopped wearing one of my favorite dresses. Anxiety sucks!

Now into my early sixties, my private psychotherapy practice consists mainly of clients over fifty with second half of life issues. In this final phase of life, there are common issues for any of us who have now made it to this place of being.

"The curious paradox is that when I accept myself just as I am, then I can change." Carl Rogers

Carl Rogers was a humanist psychologist who believed that for humans to grow, an environment of genuineness, acceptance and empathy is needed. Carl Jung, the Swiss psychiatrist who founded analytical psychology, had different ideas about the psyche. Jung said, "Neurosis is always a substitute for legitimate suffering."

One definition of neuroses is a set of functional mental disorders that cause distress but do not manifest delusions or hallucinations, and whereby behaviors are not outside socially acceptable norms.

While my approach is a humanistic one, it is also one that allows the suffering to access healing. So, while those "neurotic" behaviors may not be outside of socially acceptable patterns, our internal anxiety meter can feel as if we could blow a worry gasket at any moment. That gasket that shows up in our peripheral vision is something that we may see that no one else can. Anxiety can make us believe we are having delusional thoughts.

Remember that roommate? Anxiety sucks!

In 2005, Dixie, the last in a long line of our golden retrievers, died. My husband forced a Chihuahua mix puppy on me as a replacement. We named her Nada, the perfect description for the little bit of nothing she was. While this little nothing of a dog took to my husband, she and I were anxious and afraid of each other. I wondered if I was transferring my anxieties to her. She would growl and snip at me if I came near as she sat on my husband's lap. I decided either she had to go, or I had to get over my anxiety.

The solution was found in Marilyn Nichols, a dog whisperer who taught Nada and me how to get along. Marilyn trained people and taught dogs tricks. Her training of us included putting Nada in the submissive pose to relieve her of any anxiety or fears. Once I allowed myself to feel the fear of seeing my dog on the ground growling with me hovering over her, my anxieties were dispelled along with Nada's. It was because of that training that Nada and I experienced a joyous and transformative moment. That in-the-moment experience was so significant to me that I felt compelled to write about it. My transformation came from the insight I gained writing about my lifelong insecurities and anxieties.

The revelation was the immense gratitude I began to have for all those moments. When I explored my past struggles and found my own truths, my perspective of my past shifted. I no longer felt a need to see my life through rose-colored glasses or to deny any hurts that I experienced. No longer did I have to think about any past hurts as suffering. My life made sense to me, and I was blessed to be a part of the whole story.

My writing journey was so therapeutic that I want to help you experience your joys, gratitude, peace, and healing from anxieties through exploration of **your** truths. This self-exploration will bring you to a place of acceptance, well-being, and joy by overcoming many of your past and future anxieties. I want to help you find your voice along with ways to a more joyful you, even with the anxieties of our time.

Begin to explore the following questions. You may find your answers in this guide.

CALL TO ACTION QUESTIONS

1. What brings about my worries?

2. How can I accept my anxiety about getting older?

3. How can I stop taking comments so personally?

4. How can I feel empowered instead of powerless over my worries?

5. How can I forgive that person for what he or she did?

6. How can I forgive myself for past regrets?

7. How can I stop ruminating about the past, and worrying about the future?

8. How can I stop worrying about things over which I have no control?

9. How can I become grateful for what I do have and not hope for more?

10. How can I find joy in life with such huge worries?

11. How can I stop worrying so much about my death and the death of others I love?

2

WHAT, ME WORRY?

"The psychological condition of fear is divorced from any concrete and true immediate danger. It comes in many forms: unease, worry, anxiety, nervousness, tension, dread, phobia, and so on. This kind of psychological fear is always of something that might happen, not of something that is happening now."

Eckhart Tolle, *The Power of Now*

If you ever have been labelled a worrywart, you may worry that your anxiety is out of proportion to someone else's anxiety. You may worry that you worry too much. You may be in a constant state of anxiety about what *might* happen to you, or someone else. Maybe you are focused on all the negative things that happened in your past. You may wonder if any or all of this is normal.

In fact, most people who come into therapy for anxiety, and even depression, want to know that they are not going crazy, because that is a major, common, frequent and natural concern. Common questions are, "Is this normal worry?" "Can I recover from this?" "Will I lose my mind?" "Am I crazy for feeling this way or having these thoughts?" and even, "Am I normal?"

What is normal worry versus abnormal worry, anyway?

Karen Swartz, M.D., Director of Clinical Programs at the John Hopkins Mood Disorders Center, reports that the difference between normal worry and more serious worry such as someone with a generalized anxiety disorder is the amount of *time* spent in worry. Someone with a normal amount of worry might focus on their past or future concerns an hour a day. But someone labeled with an anxiety disorder might worry an average of up to five hours a day. Maybe more.

That is a lot of time spent in either the past or the future. Think of what else you could be doing with all that time without getting your heart rate up, gritting your teeth, biting your nails, and focusing on the "what ifs."

Alfred E. Neuman was a fictional character, a mascot for the magazine *Mad* that started in the 50's. At one point they would put the word "idiot" under his face. His motto was, *What, me worry?* This irreverent magazine that was revolutionary for its time made me think about how they chose that motto. I used to believe that their thinking was, "You would have to be an idiot not to worry about your life."

It wasn't until my mother died eleven years ago that I thought about how the gulf between my own death and me had grown shallower. I began to worry about my own end of life. A peer had expressed a similar thought to me as a way of offering sympathy for my loss. Her mother had died years before.

"Now," she told me, "there is no one left to keep us from our own demise; after our parents die, *that's it.*" I remember thinking how unsympathetic she sounded. But when I really listened to the new awareness she had gained, I realized that this was her sincere struggle for words of comfort.

She was right. After our parents die, the safety net is gone and we are next in line. Until she offered me her observations, my own death was the furthest thing from my mind. I had only been focused on what kind of life I would have without my mom around. But now I had my mom's death to grieve and my own death to worry about.

It is pretty common in this second half of our lives to wonder, "How much time do I have left? Is this the last time I will see my sister, brother, child, grandparent, uncle, aunt, spouse, friend?" You don't want anything to happen to yourself, but your biggest fear is that something will happen to someone you love.

If you stand in any line at a coffee shop, at an airport, or at work, you may hear someone end a phone conversation with "Love you." We don't want to miss an opportunity to send our love out, letting a special person know we care. It will be difficult enough to live without a person we have loved throughout our lives. Not letting them know how much we care could mean living with guilt forever.

This time factor is a major source of anxiety.

Statistics from the American Psychological Association show that more than eleven percent of adults over fifty-five suffer from anxiety disorders. That is one in every nine adults. These statistics account just for the people who are anxious enough to respond to surveys.

Who expects anxiety to take center stage in the second half of our lives? Aren't we supposed to be calm, peaceful, happy, joyful and contented at this time of our life? Instead, if you have experienced anxiety throughout your life, you may find that your worries linger and even increase.

"How can a person deal with anxiety? You might try what one fellow did. He worried so much that he decided to hire someone to do his worrying for him. He found a man who agreed to be his hired worrier for a salary of $200,000 per year. After the man accepted the job, his first question to his boss was, "Where are you going to get $200,000 per year?"

To which the man responded, "That's your worry." — Max Lucado

Sometimes you don't even realize just how anxious you are. It can be so second nature that before you know it, you are stressed out and frazzled. How many of you can relate to some of the anxiety in the following example?

Say you are driving down the highway pondering the time it will take you to get through the line at Café au Lately and still be on time for work. You don't go to that large coffee house chain because you find the coffee bitter and the lines too long. You're listening to KWHOA 290 FM and the radio blasts "In a New York Minute" by The Eagles. Singing along, you think what a nice soothing melody it is. *"In a New York minute, everything can change ...Johnny got up, dressed all in black went down to the station, and he never came back."*

Whoa—he never came back? *"If you find someone to love you better hang on tooth and nail,"* the Eagles sing.

You wonder if there is some psychic message in this song meant just for you:

Why am I hearing this song at this moment while I am driving at a high rate of speed and this guy in front of me is going soooo slow? Man, it's true—anything can happen. I need to change my will. We left all our extra money to our neighbors Frieda and oh, what's his name, her husband that helped Aunt Betty during her cancer treatment? But we've moved five times since then. What was the name of that street we lived on? And what extra money? It's all gone now because that financial advisor we met in line at Costco said, "Put it in stocks." We might as well have dumped it in the toilet.

What was that jerk's name? Why did we listen to him? Shoot, I better call my mother-in-law and tell her I love her because life is just too damn short....Where's my phone? Damn it all, it slipped under the seat, I can still see out the windshield, I'll just kick it over close to my left leg where I can pick it up. There it is.

Wait, did I just say "Damn it all?" That's what my mother used to say. I never say that. Is she calling me or coming to get me to take me to that place we go after we die? Is this serendipity, a coincidence, or maybe a sign from God? What is going on with me? Am I going crazy or what?

No. It's just a song about how life can end in the blink of an eye. Or is it?

Anxiety, oh joy!

MYTHS ABOUT ANXIETY

One of the myths about anxiety is that labeling, or identifying a particular type of anxiety with a diagnosis, is necessary to treat it. Labeling is not necessary to treat anxiety as there are several techniques that can treat the symptoms without an opinion of whether you have a specific phobia, panic disorder, or generalized anxieties.

Yet, there are times when it can be helpful.

Labeling anxious behavior to give it a diagnosis may be helpful if you are a doctor who follows the medical model whose tenets are Assess, Diagnose, and Treat with medication to alleviate the symptoms caused by the problems to which we have just given a diagnosis. If you go into a medical doctor's office such as your primary care doctor or to the emergency room with shortness of breath, heart palpitations, trembling or shaking, chest pain or discomfort or a fear of dying, you will be checked out and given a finding.

Panic symptoms can mimic heart problems and when you are having a panic attack, you may believe you are having a heart attack. Many people go to a medical facility with panic attacks thinking they are on the verge of dying and instead find out that the symptoms they were having were in fact anxiety related.

Some doctors will prescribe anti-depressants, which can be very helpful and often are used as the first line of medical treatment for anxiety. However, anti-anxiety medication, or benzodiazepines, can be addictive. Without proper guidance, education, and follow up, you can find yourself with an additional problem on your hands.

I have had several anxious clients who were fearful of taking any medications because of all the side effects. When you look at the possible problems that can go awry while taking a medication compared with one symptom being *anxiety*, well, the neurotic within us tells us we would rather have the tried and true familiar anxiety instead of the unknown one.

There are some disorders which may be extremely helpful to diagnose. Post-Traumatic Stress Disorder, or PTSD, is one of those. Until the newest diagnostic manual came out, it was under the Anxiety Disorders category. Labeling for PTSD may be helpful for someone who does not experience symptoms of flashbacks, nightmares, startled response, or extreme panic until many months or years after the event.

When you are informed that this is what you are experiencing and it is called PTSD due to a war event, abuse, accident, or some other trauma, it is normalized. You can then treat it. It can be helpful for someone to hear how common and understandable their reactions are based on past or recent past incidents. You may feel validated that you are not going crazy but are having symptoms from a very real mental illness.

Depression, which often goes hand in hand with anxiety, can also be very helpful to identify. Many people who experience symptoms of depression—lack of concentration, difficulty sleeping, loss of appetite, feeling overwhelmed, preoccupation with worry, uncontrollable crying, or suicidal thoughts—may be unaware of what is happening to them. They just know they feel helpless or hopeless.

Often a family member notices a change in behaviors before the individual experiencing the symptoms does. And once these symptoms are identified as depression, you can start to get the help you need to improve.

Diagnosing a set of symptoms can be helpful if someone is having psychotic symptoms, as in hallucinations or delusional thinking. Yet, once a diagnosis is given, symptoms are often seen within those parameters, which may not always be useful in getting someone the help they need. Sometimes just looking at the possible causes of the symptoms can help.

Well-known psychiatrist Dr. Milton Erickson often treated patients diagnosed with psychotic disorders. Jay Haley, a founding father of both brief and family therapies, wrote in his book, *Jay Haley on Milton H. Erickson,* about how Dr. Erickson was once asked to see a hospital patient who complained of frequent stomach pains after eating. The staff's thoughts were that this patient was stuck in some type of delusional thought that would benefit from Dr. Erickson's wisdom. They hoped the eminent psychiatrist would unravel this schizophrenic's sick thoughts.

Dr. Erickson talked to this patient, asked him all about his stay in the hospital and went with him to the cafeteria to check out the food. It was determined that the cafeteria food was giving this patient a stomach-ache. He was not delusional about his stomach pain. Once the food was seen as the culprit, the patient no longer complained of stomach pain.

Situations like this are why I hesitate to specifically label behaviors. As the Sigmund Freud joke goes, "Sometimes a cigar is just a cigar."

Physicians and psychiatrists utilize the medical model, which includes labeling or diagnosing a set of symptoms. Again, this can be helpful to eliminate or rule out other problems or disorders. Even for psychological symptoms, some people value learning what is going on with them so that they know they are not alone with it, that it is a real problem and not all in their head. While I don't think it is necessary to label a type of anxiety before treating it, I will briefly discuss the various anxiety disorders for informational purposes.

ANXIETY DIAGNOSES

Here are the main disorders labeled under the Anxiety Category in the DSM-V, the Diagnostic and Statistical Manuel of Mental Disorders, 5th edition.

Generalized Anxiety Disorder (GAD) – People with generalized anxiety disorder experience unrealistic, excessive, and persistent worry about issues like their health, work, money or family, for six months or longer. They don't know how to stop the worry cycle, which they feel is beyond their control.

Social Anxiety Disorder (Social Phobia) – The extreme fear of being scrutinized and judged by others in social or performance situations. The anxiety can interfere significantly with daily routines, occupational performance, or social life, making it difficult to complete school, interview and get a job, or have friendships and romantic relationships.

Panic Disorder – Panic disorder is diagnosed in people who experience spontaneous, seemingly out-of-the-blue panic attacks and who are preoccupied with the fear of a recurring attack. Panic attacks occur unexpectedly, sometimes even waking you up in the middle of your sleep.

Agoraphobia – This anxiety disorder is characterized as fear of public places, yet can be fear of vast open areas, crowdedness, as in a shopping mall or an outdoor concert, or fear of airports, bridges or other uncontrolled settings.

Phobias – A persistent fear of a circumscribed stimulus whereby the exposure almost invariably provokes an immediate anxiety response. The common ones are exposure to snakes, insects and rodents, heights, flying, closed spaces, needles, or witnessing a blood-related injury.

Selective Mutism – A rare type of anxiety disorder whose main characteristic is the failure to speak in specific social situations where speaking is expected, despite talking in other situations.

And though, like PTSD, **Obsessive Compulsive Disorder,** or OCD, is no longer under the category of Anxiety Disorders, it is often all about anxiety. If you have obsessions or persistent ideas, thoughts or impulses, the way you may prevent any further discomfort, or at least reduce any further anxiety about those thoughts, might be to compulsively repeat certain behaviors. You can think of it like a canceling out of those unrelenting thoughts. Some statistics claim that as many as one in fifty people have OCD. It can be debilitating to sufferers. Yet, there is treatment for it and one very successful treatment is "Tapping", which I talk more about later in this chapter and for which there is a demonstration exercise in the appendix.

If you want more information about any of these disorders or if you have other questions you can ask your health provider or go to your health provider's website. The Internet has a lot of information about each one, but stay away from blogs unless you want to participate in a lot of misinformed chats, which may make you anxious and more nervous.

Another myth about anxiety is that you can tell yourself you are not anxious. When you are experiencing a state of anxiety with negative self-talk, rapid shallow breathing, sweaty palms, shakiness or trembling, you may say, "I am not anxious, I don't want to be anxious, and I am okay, or I will be okay."

This often makes us more anxious.

One of the ways we deal with our worries is to deny them, or at least deny that we can't deal with them. We might tell ourselves, "Stop worrying; that will never happen." Or "I am not anxious about this upcoming surgery. It's not helpful to be worried; it's only going to make things worse." Or "I can handle this. No big deal."

Actually, studies have shown that people who expressed their anxiety before a surgery did better overall after the surgery than people who said they weren't afraid. We often deny that we are scared silly of experiencing illness and loss, our own and that of a loved one, our grief over a death, our own loneliness. It can all just become too much to bear.

We can become stoic. We don't show our feelings, we endure pain, we don't complain and we do this, we say, for the people around us. If a friend or family member has just received a life-threatening diagnosis, we don't discuss it. We think if they want to talk about it they will. We think, *I can handle this. By not talking about this reality, I maintain my composure.*

Yes, until you no longer can.

Another way we deny our anxiety is to become addicted to something, anything, to circumvent our worries and fears. We drink excessively, overmedicate, overwork, shop until we drop, become porn, Internet or video game addicts. Fear, worry and apprehension about the future or obsessive thoughts about something painful in our past can scare the heck out of us. We will do anything not to feel it. We are afraid to succumb to the pain of the self-defeating negative thoughts that bring anxiety to the forefront of our minds, which can take over and render us immobilized with fear.

"To be beautiful means to be yourself. You don't need to be accepted by others. You need to accept yourself." — ThichN-hatHanh

Instead of denying you have any anxiety, if you are nervous or worried about something like an upcoming event, ask yourself, "What is this about? What am I saying to myself that is causing this thought that keeps me in anxious knots?" Talk to your body, acknowledge the worry, fear, self-doubt, and breathe into it. Accept the feeling of nervousness, and breathe.

You may even say out loud, "I am really feeling nervous right now." It is important to accept the feeling and the tension that goes along with it, without judging it.

Take a deep breath in through the nose, hold for five to six seconds, then exhale deeply through your mouth. Do this for several breaths, though not enough to hyperventilate. Notice what you are saying to yourself along with how nervous you are feeling.

It will probably be something like, "I can't do this, I am not good enough, I don't know what I am doing, or I feel worthless, inadequate, or stupid."

Acknowledge any thoughts you are having—let your body know you get it. When you can do this, you are being in the present moment, and the anxiety dissipates.

Another myth about anxiety is that the way to treat it is the same throughout the life stages. A lot of clinicians and alternative caregivers treating anxiety will offer brief therapies, or solution-focused goals, which can offer symptomatic relief. There is nothing wrong with these methods and often they can be very effective and helpful. In fact, brief therapies are a large part of how I work with anxiety.

Each therapist, clinician, healer, or health worker will use the techniques they believe will rid you of the anxiety you have. In the first stage of life, it might be very helpful to patch someone up with coping skills that can be useful in certain situations.

Yet, when anxiety *doesn't* go away, or you continue to have the same fears return, especially in this stage of life, it is time to offer a new perspective on those fears. Most likely, some past event or events are still troubling you, and you must get to the source of your pain and suffering. This is where writing can be so effective to help you get to the core of what is bothering you, shaming you and keeping you stuck with negative thoughts about yourself and your life.

Many of my own anxieties dissipated once I wrote about the times that brought up an insecurity or worry. For instance, I used to have a fear of signing my name in public, either on a credit card receipt or on a business document such as a mortgage or a will. My hand would shake and tremble and the fear of identifying myself to the public would terrify me. Each time I had to sign my name in front of others,

I believed that I would be seen as an incompetent fraud. I worried that others were thinking, *How can this woman help others with their anxiety when she shakes like a leaf just signing her name?*

My understanding of this fear came after writing about how I was punished as a child. Growing up, any type of candy or sweet was my way to soothe and calm my anxiety and worry over any household chaos. If I was caught finding a candy stash and eating some of it, my mother would tell me to wait until my father got home for my punishment. For hours before he arrived home, I was in a state of nerves and anxious apprehension.

Once my father arrived back at our house and after hearing the story of my misdeed from my mother, I would hear what felt like fatal words from my father.

"Put out your hand."

I'd cringe and do what I was told. I remember feeling so ashamed that I could do something so bad as to warrant this greeting. Instead of a warm hug, or acknowledgment of my presence, I was scolded for eating candy; that treat that I used to relieve my anxieties that was now causing me further anxiety.

Early on I learned not to feel comfortable in my own skin so when I had to present myself to others, I expected harsh consequences. That early form of punishment became a breeding ground for my irrational anxiety.

I may still have the thought at times of, *What if I shake while signing my name?* When that does occur, I think, *Well, so be it. My hand is shaking.* Because I no longer see myself as incompetent, I don't perceive that from others and I can separate any negative thoughts from the action.

If you are familiar with anxiety from the first half of life, you may continue to believe that you must consider all the possible computations of "what ifs," a ruminating, obsessive style of worrying, an inner rant of negative thoughts.

What if *I fail, fall apart, throw up, have a heart attack, let someone see me shake, or go crazy?* You may believe that it is helpful to imagine all the consequences a particular behavior or action may have before you complete it.

If this is you, it is important to ask yourself, "What is the worst that can happen?" These worries that used to seem as though we were doing something about the possibility of something happening by worrying have become useless to us. The worry will not help, and takes you out of the present moment and into a state of fear. If you have these types of worry, you must ask yourself, "What is my worst fear?" Then explore it, write about it, and let it go.

If your greatest fear is that you could die, or someone you love could die, and you ruminate over when this fear will happen, it is time to let go. This is not the time of life to spend worrying about "what ifs."

You can also set aside a worry time. If you find you worry more often than not, set aside twenty minutes at the same time each day to worry. If something comes up which starts to worry you, save it for today's worry time, or for tomorrow's. You can then be present for the rest of your day rather than lost in past or future thoughts.

In graduate school another student and I offered a free group on "Fear of Public Speaking." Because of our own fears about presenting in front of groups, we decided to rid ourselves of those fears while we helped others with it at the same time.

We held this group in a small space off the therapy rooms at a clinic where one of the other social work students had her internship. We placed an ad in the local newspaper and once we found a following of nine other students, we began the group we had hoped would rid us of our fears as well as the fears of the other trusting members.

One of the questions we asked a group member was, "What is the worst thing you fear could happen during a speech?" A young male member said that his greatest fear was that he would throw up. When I asked if that had ever happened he said that it had. He described a talk in which he got up to speak, looked out at the audience, and then walked away to vomit minutes later.

I remember that all of us, including the co-facilitator, were silent. We didn't know what to say.

If his worst fear had come true, then "Now what?" What comfort or help could we offer to convince him that it wouldn't happen again? He was so frightened that it might reoccur that he would not get up in front of our group to talk further about it. He told us this as we went around the room sharing our worst fears.

Sadly, he never returned for any more of our unprofessional assistance. His fear may or may not have actually happened. He was distrustful that we could help, and he may have been testing us to see how we would respond.

Yet, despite whether he was being truthful, now I would offer him different questions, and different options. I had not delved into his background and do not know if something from his past could be involved. A question may be, "So that is no longer your worst fear?" or, "Is your worst fear now that the audience would find that out?"

My more trained thoughts are that once we knew that fear about him had come to fruition, if it truly had, he felt shame for exposing himself in front of us. Many people there knew that we were social workers in training, not yet full-fledged clinicians, which led to a high amount of attrition. We may have had a better success rate had we just been individuals with a fear of speaking publicly who wanted to start a support group.

TAPPING TO HEAL FROM ANXIETY

Thought Field Therapy or EFT (Emotional Freedom Technique), now often referred to as "Tapping," has its early origins in acupuncture as a way to treat physical problems through needles placed on meridians of the body. Dr. Roger Callahan, a psychologist who specialized in anxiety disorders, found that by tapping on those same energy meridians of the body in a specific way, or *algorithm* as he called it, you could completely eliminate the feelings associated with the negative thoughts you were experiencing. This particular technique is used to treat physical pain as well as psychological issues and is having a resurgence of popularity in the field of psychology.

Tapping is a wonderful tool that can help with many different issues. I have used it with various different obsessions, compulsions, and phobias. Delving into the possible origins of obsessive thoughts, compulsions, or phobias may be helpful to identify the source of any fears, but when it does not decrease the anxiety that arises, then tapping can often be very helpful.

Yes, anxiety is different in this stage of life. But you may be feeling that your anxiety now is just as bad as the first stage of life, and now you feel worse about yourself, especially since I have told you how different it is *supposed* to be in this second stage of life.

That's okay, because if you are one whose anxieties linger and have not lessened, and now you have first stage of life anxieties as well as second stage of life worries, the exercises in these chapters will help you identify what might be the breeding ground for those worries and fears. Don't forget to check out the Tapping technique at the end of the book.

ACTION PLAN

1. Have you ever been labeled as a worrywart? Do you see yourself that way?

2. Have you been given an anxiety diagnosis?

3. Was it helpful to be given this label? If so, how so? If not, why not?

4. What are some of your most pressing worries?

5. What have you done in the past to help relieve your anxiety? Was it helpful?

6. Is your anxiety at this time of your life different than in the first half of life? If so, how so?

7. What story do you tell yourself about your anxiety?

8. What story would you like to tell yourself about your anxiety?

3

GRATEFUL LIVING

"Boomers will eventually have to accept that it is not possible to stay forever young or to stop aging. But it is possible, by committing to show up for others in community after community, to earn a measure of immortality."

Eric Liu

"What a long strange trip it's been."

The Grateful Dead

Each generation is identified by decades that brought them together because of a common cause, which for the past three generations was a war. For our grandparents it was World War I, triggered by the assassination of the Archduke of Austria, where the world's great economic powers fought against other countries' political beliefs. Our parents came together to fight anti-Semitism during the forties that again involved multiple countries in the next Great War, World War II. Our own generation was brought together by a much different conflict.

The Vietnam War, an unwanted, maligned war, ripped our country into many different factions; it tore us apart and brought us together at the same time. Through all the turmoil of the 50's, 60's and 70's, the decades in which this war occurred, it is important for us aging hipsters to look back at both the anxieties of that era and the perks of aging grace-fully now. By looking back at our past, we can diminish the anxiety we may be feeling about getting older; by accepting the present moment, we can discover the joys we have in our lives now.

In these past generations there was a commonality of fight-ing for one's life, fighting for the world even. Typically, when a war ended, there was celebration; men and women returned to their lives as heroes.

For us, once the Vietnam War was over, we absorbed the loss and the remains of the soldiers who returned. No tri-umphs or celebrations, just picking up the pieces from the anti-war music that still reverberated in our heads.

"There's a man with a gun over there, a telling me I got to beware....."Buffalo Springfield, "For What It's Worth."

While the 60's and the 70's are the decades which changed our own generation the most, that time was fraught with anxiety and fears. The mantra is probably best captured in the words of Dr. Timothy Leary, a Harvard Ph.D., who re-searched human consciousness while under the influence of hallucinogens—"Turn on, Tune in, and Drop out!" This spoke of turning on to drugs, both marijuana and hallucinogens, tuning in to music that led to an inner awakening, and drop-ping out of mainstream society.

Hippies, also known as flower children for the peaceful universality that flowers portrayed, were identified by long hair, smoking marijuana, free love ideals, love of rock and roll, and hallucinogenic trips. Basically, Hippies represented a rebellion against the war that was raging both in Vietnam and here in the U.S. by the conservative government in pow-er. Some were sentenced to thirty years for smoking one pot joint.

For some of us, marijuana cured our anxiety. For others it made us paranoid.

Despite being against the war, there was still anxiety that came from rebelling against the government. Some of that anxiety was from the peer pressure to be different yet at the same time conform to each other. We were hippies, or yippies, or we were on the fringe.

I tended to be on the fringe of my life without a real term to define myself. In undergraduate school in Colorado, my own anxiety never waned in this time of free love and protest. I had more inhibitions than most of my friends and couldn't experience any sense of empowerment from the common collective consciousness. Many friends felt euphoric or normal while on pot. I felt paranoid, self-conscious and without focus. My anxiety increased with each toke of a joint.

While I had different roommates in college and after, the one roommate who never left my side at this time of my life was anxiety. It stayed close by.

Having to make a class presentation could make me fraught with obsessive worry days ahead of time. Going to an anti-war demonstration and having to vocalize for whom I planned to vote in my first presidential election and why, could produce mute silences once upon my feet to talk.

One day I decided to stand up for my beliefs against the war and confront my fears of speaking during a group. I attended a twenty-person rally held on the lawn amongst the grand old oak trees that faced our university administration building. The group was led by an assistant professor in sociology, my major. As we gathered around and sat on the grass, the professor talked about the war and why we wanted to vote against Nixon, and for the Democratic candidate, Senator George McGovern.

"Why do we want McGovern elected?" she asked the group. Before any thought took place, I realized I was waving my hand with great gusto. At that moment, she called on me and asked me to stand. It was at that same moment that my roommate took over. I stood up, looked over at our leader, and then stared back at the ground. I started making circles with my three-inch cork clogs in the fine dirt between the pockets of grass.

After what seemed like an eternity, our leader called on someone else while I sank to the ground in humiliation. My thoughts were focused on what I might have to say after "Because he is against the war." I was afraid that she might ask me anything further about why we wanted him to be president. My brain got stuck on the possibility of future humiliation and I froze.

That humiliation stayed with me for a long time. I focused on how stupid I must be for being so nervous as to not be able to speak at all, like a selective mute. If you had any phobias or anxiety during that time you may relate to this. Or you may have some other anxiety from that decade that continues to bother you, maybe even consume you. When I wrote about this story, it was easier to let it go than to hold on to it.

We may have outgrown those old obsessions about what we did back then and have moved on to seeing some of the benefits of aging. Now we are expected to live well into our nineties and beyond. Yet we don't know what that will look like and we have so many questions.

Some people say that being in our sixties is the new forties, or even thirties, though on some days with some joint pain here and muscle pain there, it can seem like the 60's are the new 90's. However you might feel on any given day, we are expected to live much longer than our parents' generation, that "greatest generation," the ones who had lived through the Roaring Twenties and the Depression and who fought in a war that changed the world, not like our war, which shamed the nation.

My mother would tell the story of when she was nineteen and in the military. She was asked by a man on the street (she never elaborated whether this man was a reporter taking a poll or just some man wanting to ask an invasive question to an attractive lady), "How *old* is old to you? What age do you want to live to be?" My mother replied with great assurance, "I don't want to live past thirty. That is old enough for me."

Her comments are reminiscent of Abbie Hoffman's rants of "Never trust anyone over thirty," which he altered once reaching that landmark age to "Never trust anyone *under* thirty." Turning thirty was the beginning of the end.

Getting older can be laden with anxieties and worries. We look in the mirror and think, *Who is that person? Not anyone I recognize.* We may feel as we did in our thirties, but we don't look thirty. Any high school or college reunions we attend are laced with fewer friends; some are too ill to attend, some have passed on, others don't want to face their differences in the mirror of their peers' faces.

If we do go back to our old schools, we look at the wrinkled and sagging skin, turkey necks, and larger bulk of these folks who used to be in the same classroom as ours and think, *My, but they have aged. Who are those people?*

Those people are now us.

So what *are* the perks of aging? How can aging be seen as a positive thing? How do we not think of it as a fast track to the end of our lives? How can we have less anxiety and find more peace and joy as we age?

For one, you are alive. The greatest gift you have been given is the gift of life. Your parents, no matter who they were or what they did for you, or to you, gave you life. That is a plus. The rest is up to us.

We must clear the path of any old anger, hurt or resentments. If you felt mistreated, abused, or neglected, you have to let go of that to make room for the true joy that can only come by acknowledging the suffering and pain, then letting go and making peace.

Peace is what we all sought during those decades of the Vietnam War.

Peace of mind is what we seek now.

If you are a baby boomer you have made it to the second half of your life. How many friends, family members, associates, colleagues in this same age group have not? How many friends became addicted to drugs, alcohol, and prescription medicine and succumbed either by accident or intentional death? How many of your friends have died of AIDS when the new cocktail of drugs was not available? How many died from that stigma of hidden and latent sexual identities? How many were shamed by that societal stigma and disgrace for being different?

And now, how many of us have hidden our true selves from society and from *ourselves?*

This time is a time to come out to the world, to be yourself, to embrace those shameful parts. To know that we are okay, no matter how we think or feel.

For women this is a time for menopause, a time when a woman's menstrual cycles decline. A woman gets to experience the full cyclone of menopausal symptoms before that living, breathing menopausal persona withers and comes to a close. For men, this can be a time to rejoice as well. After all these years of *patiently* tolerating your wife's menstrual symptoms, you can now look forward to having your sweet wife back. Right, men?

Whew! The end of the sweats for us all.

As years of mood swings, hot flashes, dried-up female parts, and our absent-mindedness come to a close, it is a time for us to reflect on our past. And while this reflection won't happen until after we get through the symptoms, once it's over, it's over. As a friend once expressed joy in words, "Pom Poms, Sparklers, and Fireworks!"

The only way out is through. Do you remember the saying that so many women with Premenstrual Syndrome, or PMS, could identify with? "I've got PMS, and I've got a gun." Now with all the school shootings and lack of gun control, the line has lost its absurdity. Yet, if we changed that to, "I'm in menopause and I am hot, bloated, overweight with a mouth on me," one may understand.

Sex matters. It matters especially during this time of our lives. Physical intimacy can keep us connected to our spouse and add to the emotional intimacy of the aging experience. The sex is different, more intimate, slower, and less acrobatic, if it ever was. You don't have to hang from the chandelier to have great sex.

There is no more pregnancy concern or counting days between monthly periods, which can make physical intimacy less worrisome. No more forgetting to take a small pill from a round container three weeks out of the month, or to have foam, a patch or a condom nearby.

No more mood swings or fits of anger (at least that we can excuse by the curse), or extra pounds (at least due to bloat and extra water weight). Dr. Christine Northrup, author of *The Wisdom of Menopause,* tells us how this is a time of reflection, a time to look back and see from where we have come, what we really want now for our lives. It is a time to live, be, and do just what we want to do.

Period. The end.

We are not focusing on whether or not to have children, how to raise our kids, being laid off or being fired. Though having work is still a huge concern to support ourselves and to save for any retirement, it is different. Retirement takes on a new meaning. Some of us will never voluntarily retire or stop working. This may be for money reasons or because we are passionate about our work, or both.

But it is a different worry. We no longer worry about making sure we have enough to support our children, their education, or their failed starts at work, just ourselves and our spouse or partner, or maybe helping out a parent in need. Time is more of a factor than anything. We don't want to outlive our money, but we want to live long enough to spend it.

Medicare, our universal health plan, is available at sixty-five, and Social Security at sixty-two, sixty-seven or seventy, depending on when you decide to take the supplemental monies into which we all paid. We get discounts on movie tickets, airline fares, car rentals, hotels, restaurants. You may not be aware of many of the very practical discounts you can receive, but you can find more information on the Internet.

Rhonda, a client who is an oil painter, beamed as she described her joy at taking classes from a top-notch artist for a third of what it would cost her if she were not sixty-five. As a retired government employee, she also receives a pension which allows her the ability to not have to worry about finances.

These small discounts may not seem as far out to you, as you may still have large amounts of debt and money woes. Realize though that you will always have financial concerns, so it is important to explore how you can limit them, and then work on the inner consciousness that you can change from worry to *in-the-moment* peace.

All of these woes and worries that occur in our fifties, six-ties, and beyond are normal. Erik Erikson, a developmental psychologist, developed a theory of eight stages of psychoso-cial development, and writes about these stages in *Identity and the Life Cycle*.

He discusses how each stage comes with a conflict, and what he calls a Resolution or "Virtue."

1. Infancy, ages 0-1 year — Trust vs. Mistrust/ Hope

2. Early childhood, 1 to 3 years — Autonomy vs. Shame and Doubt/Will

3. Play age, 3-6 years — Initiative vs. Guilt/Pur-pose

4. School Age, 6-12 years — Industry vs. Inferi-ority/Competence

5. Adolescence, 12-19 years — Identity vs. Con-fusion/Fidelity

6. Early Adulthood, 20-39 years — Intimacy vs. Isolation/Love

7. Adulthood, 40 – 64 years — Generativity vs. Stagnation/Care

8. Age 65 through one's death — Integrity vs. Despair/Wisdom

These stages don't necessarily follow a consecutive pattern and not all of us find our way in or out of these stages. Some-times we don't come to the resolution that Erikson promis-es. Though by the time we pass into our sixties, there is of-ten some inkling that we need to focus on productivity and well-being.

His seventh stage of development is labeled "Generativity vs. Stagnation" and encompasses the ages from forty to sixty-five. During this time of life, we might be rebuilding our careers, being productive in our hobbies and interests, and finding new outlets for our inner desires.

I met my old friend Toni when she was just out of college and was working as a dental hygienist. After six years of cleaning teeth, she went to hairdresser's school to become a hair stylist. She worked part time in a salon while her kids grew up and I'd often go to her house for haircuts. After her interest in cutting hair waned, she went back to school, got her Master's in Education and began teaching fourth grade, which lasted three years, as the hours were long and pay was low. She needed to spread her wings again.

Now at age sixty-four, she is in her seventeenth year with a well-known real estate office close to her home. It offers her flexibility, good income and she says she has the most reasonable boss she's ever had—herself. Another career may be in her future, but I think this satisfies her need for flexibility, and the ability to make a good income. It is never too late to find a satisfying vocation or hobby.

Erikson's theory proposes the virtue associated with this seventh stage as "Care." We may be settled in a relationship and developing a sense of being a part of the bigger picture. We are giving back, helping, contributing, maybe involved in the community or volunteering. If we fail to achieve these objectives according to Erikson, we can become stagnant and feel unproductive.

The last stage of his theory is for those sixty-five or older. He calls this stage "Ego Integrity vs. Despair." The term *senior citizen* is often applied, our productivity slows down and we may be exploring life as a retired person. Of course, because our system has changed so much since the decade in which we grew up, many of us who worked entire lives at the same company no longer have the expected pensions and need to continue to work.

But we are starting to ponder our achievements. We can develop integrity if we are able to see our successes. Erikson says that if we see our lives as unproductive, feel guilt about our past, or feel that we did not accomplish our life goals, we can become dissatisfied with our lives and can develop despair, often leading to depression, hopelessness, and anxiety.

Are you feeling this way? Writing about your past will help. In the next chapters, there will be ways to explore the uniqueness and wonder of you despite your age and despite your past. You can begin to look at your accomplishments instead of what you may be seeing as failures. You can look at how your choices brought you to a place, a place right where you need to be. You can look at the silver linings that exist which you may never have found without more exploration of your past and where you are at this moment.

A recent study on psychedelic mushrooms, shrooms or magic mushrooms, as they were commonly called in the 60's, published in *Human Brain Mapping,* co-authored by Dr. Robin Carhart-Harris, a researcher in Neuro psychopharmacology at Imperial College London, produced some interesting results. A mind-altering compound found in hundreds of mushroom species is being explored as a potential treatment for some anxiety and depression.

The belief is that the drugs will allow for mental exploration and can produce more optimism about life, less self-centeredness and more happiness months after the "trip." Instead of treating anxiety and depression with medications that numb and dampen emotions, the researchers are expressing real benefits from unlocking emotions and opening up one's mind to promote more positive and permanent change in one's self and world views.

Some of you may be thinking, *Far out, Dude!*

While I am not advocating taking shrooms to enhance a more positive worldview, this study seems to validate how the process of a successful self-exploration in this stage will lead to the virtue of wisdom. Wisdom enables us to look back on our life with a sense of closure and completeness, and to also accept death without fear.

Here are some questions only you can answer. These are the questions upon which it will be helpful for you to journal.

ACTION PLAN

1. What were the 60's like for you? If you are male, did you go to Vietnam? Were you a draft dodger, or conscientious objector? Or maybe you sought a college deferment, or asked a doctor to find some malady so you could find a way out of the draft? How about your mate?

2. Was this an anxious time for you? If so, how?

3. Did you consider yourself a passivist, a hippie? An activist or Yippie? Maybe you were on the perimeter, focused on college, in a sorority or fraternity. What kind of impact did this time of your life have on you? What impact does it have for you now?

4. What does getting older mean to you? Do you feel that you are getting better? If so, in what ways? What do you see as the perks of aging?

5. What is your greatest accomplishment in your life so far?

6. One additional question for you. If you got a tattoo at this time of your life, what would it be? If you have one now, do you regret getting it? Or would you get the same one all over again?

4

Don't Take It Personally, But That Anxiety Is All About You

"Whatever happens around you, don't take it personally.... Nothing other people do to you is because of you. It is because of themselves."

Don Miguel Ruiz

"The whole theory of the universe is unerringly directed towards one single individual – namely to you."

Walt Whitman

Anything other people say to you is about them. Anything you say or do to someone else is about you. While we can say that nothing other people say to us is about us personally, our thoughts will make it seem as if it is so. The only part that is personal in this very impersonal equation is how you interpret someone's words and how you choose to respond. When you take something personally, it then becomes all about you again. For when you take someone else's words to heart and let them get to your very core, you can become anxious and afraid, worried that those words are true.

"Sticks and stones may break my bones but words will never harm me."

Remember this old adage that we all used to say in taunting to a bully who just said something mean or hurtful? Maybe it was a sibling that called you a "rat" for telling on them, or called you a "creep," or worse, used words that were true, like "fat" or "short," or words that you thought of yourself to be true like "stupid" or "dumb."

Those words did hurt, darn it, and they hurt badly. Words sting like alcohol to a sore, or a stake to the heart. As youngsters, we have yet to build a protective shell around our heart and we can *feel* words pierce our inner sanctum and give credence to what we already assumed was true.

Taking what someone says to us as truth is a first stage of life conflict. Letting another's assessment of us bother us is something we did when we were young when we allowed peers and bullies to affect our mood. Now we need to see another's words as a reflection of them, not as a factual account of truth about us.

Don Miguel Ruiz wrote *The Four Agreements*. It is a good short book and worth the read, full of small pearls of wisdom that when heeded can be very helpful. One of the four agreements that he asks you to make is *Don't take anything personal*. This concept has become a very useful expression to remind anyone having a relationship issue with a friend, child, co-worker, neighbor, spouse, ex, boss, or even *ourselves*.

One day during a therapy session, my own, a seemingly trivial comment a friend made to me was on my mind. I brought it up to my therapist, who happens to be a very wise man. I was feeling petty for allowing a little remark to bother me and I told him so. In fact, I don't remember what this friend said to me, but I do remember well the exchange that happened later.

I told him, "This is petty. I hate feeling this way and should just move on to other more important issues, like how much time I have left in the world, right? I mean what am I doing telling you about paltry stuff when your time is precious and I am wasting it."

"Not at all, Sue. This isn't petty. This is about you," he replied.

"So are you saying I'm not being petty for bringing this up?"

"This is important to explore. It's fine. Let's talk about it."

"Yeah, but I am making this about me," as I continued to talk about me.

"It is always about you," was his astute reply.

What he was saying was that I *was* taking my peer's words personally. He wanted to explore what I was saying to *myself* about those words so that I could challenge that negative arrow I had directed towards my belief system and see it with a new, more realistic perspective.

It is that negative belief system we hold about ourselves that causes us anxiety. Depending on our past experiences, we may hear a remark as negative when it was not intended that way. When someone makes a comment to us, we may become fearful, worried, or feel shame, especially if the statement is not a positive one. Yet, how you see that comment *is* about you and needs to be challenged so that you can let go of any anxious thoughts to which you are holding on.

Most of us think that the world does not revolve around us and that we are just a measly piece of the pie that God, parents, spouse, friends, neighbors, children, pets (well pets do come before us) should come before us. We must consider others' feelings first. We must come second. We are taught to be considerate, kind, courteous, and to help other people at all times and obey the girl scout/boy scout laws. If that is truth, then we are not supposed to think of ourselves first.

Consider your neighbor first, then yourself, right?

ABOUT FACE

This may go against conventional wisdom, but the truth is the world *does* revolve around us. How we take things matters because our *response* is all about us. We see things from our vantage point due to our biological nature, our upbringing, our parents' mode of discipline (or not), birth order, education, travels, choice of studies, friends and teachers; all these and more make us who we are.

You are unique and have a perspective that no one else has. If we are true and honest with ourselves once we know what we think and feel, then our worldview is all about us. When we take care of ourselves first and learn what is important and meaningful to us, what drives us, our priorities, about what we are passionate, how to be healthy in mind and bodies, then we have so much more to offer. It is a disservice to ourselves and others around us to put someone else above us.

On the spectrum of the selfish/selfless scale it is closer to the selfish scale, as it means that you are taking care of another for your own purpose, not out of love. You cannot truly love another person completely until you know and love yourself.

When you find that love for yourself and can accept yourself, then you can love and give to another. Anything else sets us up for a codependent relationship, dependent on the needs or control of another. The codependent relationship is an excessive emotional or psychological reliance on another person.

A codependent relationship can have us taking another's remarks to heart because of our dependence on what they may say and what they may think of us. If it isn't a positive or nice assessment of how we would like to see ourselves, we can feel bad about ourselves.

For example, if your grown adult daughter tells you she hates you in a fit of rage, and the only provocation is that you told her she would need to start looking for ways to pay her own bills from now on, that hate is directed towards you and is about you as she is talking to you, as her mother, or her father. If you decide not to hold her accountable because you are fearful she will hate you for setting limits, and you continue to let her stay without consequences or limits, you are allowing your fears to guide your actions.

If you decide that you are a bad mother or father because of her remark, then that is a negative distortion. This comment has nothing to do with whether you are a bad or good parent. It simply says she does not want to take responsibility for her actions, and that she has not learned how to take care of herself.

Breaking the Cognitive Behavior Cycle

When you allow what someone else says or doesn't say, or what they do or don't do, to affect whether you feel okay about yourself, you are letting their deeds or actions upset you. You are taking their words to heart and allowing anxiety to breed.

The Cognitive Cycle states that when an event occurs, how we interpret that event can lead to negative *self-talk* like, *I am worthless, I did that wrong, I am a bad person, I am not good enough,* (fill in the blank)—which leads to *feelings* of *sadness, hurt, anxiety, worry, shame, disgust, disgrace,* (fill in the blank), which leads us to react a certain way—*yell, scream, leave, cry, retreat, get angry, act out,* (fill in the blank), which causes *consequences* of that behavior which may be for us to *isolate, have suicidal thoughts or actions, quit, leave,* (fill in the blank). If the cycle is not interrupted or changed in any way, it will continue and become a pattern.

So, anytime you *feel* anxious, worried, hurt, mad, or ashamed, explore this cycle.

Go back to the event. Notice what you said to yourself about what occurred. What were your thoughts about yourself related to that event? What were you saying to yourself at the time that made you feel that anxiety, worry, anger, hurt or shame?

The thoughts that come up are often called *automatic* thoughts. Often we are not aware of what we are thinking, just what we are feeling. To break out of this pattern, you will need to first identify the thoughts that you are having about that event. This will enable you to see how you are viewing yourself negatively. Once you can do that, you can challenge those thoughts and change them to more realistic ones. Instead of reacting to a situation, you can choose how you want to respond.

Notice what you did, how you acted or behaved when you had these negative thoughts along with that fear or anxiety. What were the consequences of those behaviors?

Let's say you are walking into your office and a co-worker passes you in the hallway. You greet him, put out your hand to shake his or to give him a pat on the shoulder, and he walks past without responding to your greeting. You might even turn around to see if he heard you, yet he continues on his way.

How would you think of this? Would you think he was angry or upset with you? That you did something wrong? That he just got fired, quit, maybe over something you caused to happen? Would you get anxious that you may have somehow triggered this response by something you did yesterday, last week, a month ago? Would you start to obsess over what you may have said or done?

Or would you think that maybe he didn't hear you, was caught up in his own world, had a bad morning, focused on a sick pet, child or grandchild, just got some bad news, or just got fired, or quit, or any other hundreds of possibilities?

If you chose the latter, then you realize that what someone does or does not do is not about you, but about them.

If you chose the former, you may be normal, as it is common to infer the worst. We all do it at times. But to continue to take it personal when someone says something to you is more of a first stage of life response. Our identity is often shaped by what we think others think of us, and of course by what we think of ourselves.

Now, we don't need to rely on other's views of us. We need to learn what we are thinking about ourselves and learn how to challenge our personal negative self-talk and reframe any self-defeating thoughts and beliefs.

Consider the way out of this cycle. If you look at every event that happens to you in a very objective way, without judgment or qualifying it as good or bad, you can get out of your own way.

Looking at the above example, the event that occurred was: you greeted a co-worker and he didn't respond. That's it. While you may think otherwise, he didn't *ignore* you, wasn't *rude* to you, didn't *spit in your face*, or *reject* you. He simply did not respond to your greeting. That was the event.

In looking at any action for what it *is*, as opposed to how you might interpret it, you can then challenge any negative thought that you might be having about yourself or what he *did to you,* and instead say to yourself, "Whoa, I wonder what is going on with Bob? Maybe I'll check it out with him later."

Or you might decide to go check it out with him now, or ask another co-worker about it. But you take the onus of responsibility off yourself. You didn't do anything. Something is going on with Bob.

You are not responsible for another's feelings, actions or behaviors, or what they say to you or to anyone else. You may feel like a target sometimes if someone says something rude about you behind your back, or to your face. But even then you do not have to respond in kind.

It helps to pause and not react. Realize that if someone is rude and it is not in response to anything you said or did to them, that they are most likely hurting inside, and need to try to hurt you, which may make them feel better about themselves. It is highly likely that any unprovoked negative comment someone makes is an outward reflection of their inner hurt and turmoil.

RELATIONSHIP ANXIETY

Our relationships with others can be our greatest source of joy, and our greatest source of anxiety and pain. How we perceive ourselves in relation to another person, and how we think they perceive us, can cause anxiety to flourish.

Whether it is our spousal or partner relationship, our parent-child or child-parent relationship, or a friendship, there are times when we are wracked with guilt, shame or anxiety over what we have done or not done.

If we have low self-esteem, which really is about not having confidence in our abilities or respect for ourselves, it's pretty hard to admire a spouse who seems to do everything right, get along with others well, and not have a care in the world. When we don't feel good about ourselves, we have a hard time feeling good about others. We might start fights, argue or be grouchy, not about anything we can put a finger on, we just are not happy with ourselves.

The key here is how we perceive or think about ourselves. That is what will determine what we think our spouse, partner, friend, or co-worker thinks about us, and ultimately how we will treat *them*. If we don't like ourselves, we will have a hard time believing that anyone else does either.

Ted and Dana came into the office for marital therapy with complaints of Dana's worries over her grown daughter, Ted's stepdaughter's, addictive behavior. Thirty-seven-year-old Cassey had difficulty holding down a job, was spending lots of time in bars, and was neglecting her household chores with her live-in boyfriend. The boyfriend had been filling Dana in on Cassey's behaviors and wanted Dana to intervene.

Ted didn't want to intervene and thought it was Cassey and her boyfriend's issue to work out. Dana was torn between her husband and her daughter and this caused arguments between them.

You can see the different relationships in this story and if you get caught up in it like Dana did, you can become very codependent trying to make everyone and every issue okay. Ted believed that Dana should not even be talking with Cassey's boyfriend. Dana believed that she had to do something to help her daughter because that was her role. Dana felt that if her daughter was not happy, she could not feel good about herself. Yet, Dana's pattern of trying to fix everything held huge consequences. Her relationship with her husband was at risk.

Dana tried to make everyone and everything in her life happy and at peace while she had difficulties staying in the moment with worry and anxiety over all her past wounds, wounds into which she chose not to delve. She continued to retraumatize herself when she could not help others be happy with their lives.

We worked on teaching Dana to set boundaries with her daughter and her daughter's boyfriend. In this case, the Serenity Prayer helped Dana understand what she could do about the situation, and what she couldn't.

The Serenity Prayer says, "God grant me the serenity to accept the things I cannot change, courage to change the things I can, and the wisdom to know the difference." It goes on to say, "Living one day at a time; enjoying one moment at a time; accepting hardships as the pathway to peace." This oft-used prayer was written by an American theologian, Reinhold Niebuhr, and has been adopted by Alcoholics Anonymous and other twelve-step groups.

This prayer can be an extremely helpful mantra to say to ourselves when we get into a situation we are trying to improve to no avail or over which we have no control. And if you do not want to use God as the prayee, you can fill it in with whatever your higher power is for you.

You can find some momentary peace in your relationships if you live by the Serenity Prayer until an old wound surfaces again and starts to keep you from being in the moment because you are still focused on some past hurts.

Long-term marriage relationship researcher John Gottman Ph.D., in his book *The Seven Principles for Making Marriage Work,* says that the most important elements in a marriage are maintaining the friendship and resolving conflicts. The main issues with resolving conflicts lie in determining whether the problems are resolvable. They may be perpetual problems without solutions, or they may be solvable problems about which you can make changes.

It is crucial to know which is which so that you can make a goal to resolve what you can, and relinquish the need to solve a problem that is perpetual and not going to change, in which case you can change your attitude and perspective about it instead. If you have issues like Dana and try to change someone else's relationship or their problems, you may be in anxious knots about it. The key to untying those knots is to use the Cognitive Thought Cycle to determine what you are saying to yourself about someone else's stuff and what you are saying about yourself for not being able to change it.

A relationship doesn't make you happy. You must find your own happiness first. If you don't know what makes you happy, where you find joy, what you like and what you don't like, now is the time to find out.

What works best for a marital relationship at this stage of life is to work on *you*. Let your partner, daughter, son, or an in-law work on him or herself. If your partner wants to take it easy in this stage of life, let them. If you think gardening would be a great hobby for your spouse to take up because you like it so much, then you keep doing it. Nagging your partner to do something you see as a priority, or as a good trait to have, is fruitless. It will only alienate you from your partner instead of draw you closer.

If you are focused on another's faults, flaws or imperfections, and this is creating a lot of anxiety in your life, you may be neglecting some self-imperfections that you don't want to identify.

FIND YOUR PEACE; LET OTHERS FIND THEIRS

No more codependency. It is about *you*, not your spouse or your children. It is about finding your joy and sharing that joy with others. This is the personal part. Figure yourself out. Let your partner do the same.

Emotional detachment from whether you can make another person happy can be a gift to yourself. If you are anxiously trying to make someone else happy, start exploring your own joys, and worry less about theirs. If it is a truth for you that it is better to give than receive, then give yourself and the world a better you by taking care of yourself first. Do for yourself what you wish others would do for themselves.

Please take this personally; with all the work you are doing to heal from past wounds and future worries, you can let go of old negative thoughts and fears and find the peace of mind you have earned.

ACTION PLAN

Writing allows us to learn what we think and feel about ourselves and the world.

How do you learn about the most important relationship you have? You write. And, by the way, if I haven't made my point in this chapter, that most important relationship is with *you*.

1. What kinds of comments do you tend to take personally?

2. How can you see a comment someone makes to you differently? What might be going on with them?

3. Have you identified some of your negative self-talk?

4. What kinds of events trigger your negative talk?

5. What are some consequences of this negative talk?

6. Have you noticed a pattern of behaviors in which you engage when you take something personally? What are the feelings you have that cause you to behave a certain way?

7. How can you be kinder to yourself by changing your negative self-talk into more realistic words about a situation?

5

HOPE IS A FOUR-LETTER WORD

"To hear the phrase 'our only hope' always makes one anxious, because it means that if the only hope doesn't work, there is nothing left."
Lemony Snicket, ,The Blank Book

"True happiness is to enjoy the present, without anxious dependence upon the future, not to amuse ourselves with either hopes or fears but to rest satisfied with what we have, which is sufficient, for he that is so wants nothing. The greatest blessings of mankind are within us and within our reach. A wise man is content with his lot, whatever it may be, without wishing for what he has not."
Lucius Annaeus Seneca, a Roman Stoic philosopher born in 4 B.C.

While it may be contrary to popular and Christian beliefs and values, hope is overrated. It can keep you in a place of somewhere else, thinking, wishing or desiring a future that takes you away from this precious life we have right now. If we want to reduce our worries about the future, find that place of peace for which we seek, and experience true joy in our life, we must let go of the place of expectancy and desire of something else and find a place of peace in the present moment.

Hope is supposed to be a virtue in the Christian faith. According to the Bible, hope is an expectation of and desire of receiving something beneficial in the future. It is also a religious belief of certainty and a positive expectation of future rewards, as in life everlasting.

Yet, for the purposes of this guide, the definition for hope that I want to use is "a desire for something and the expectation of receiving it." It is that belief of *expectation* that can be destructive. What if something we desire and seek doesn't occur?

If you hope your son or daughter becomes a doctor, for example, because you believe that doctors are successful financially and hold a certain enviable status, then what if your son or daughter instead becomes a writer, an artist, or a security guard? Or stays in academia forever? Or never graduates? Doesn't finish their master's or doctorate, and you spent all that money helping them find their way? Would you bemoan their decision? Be disappointed?

What if you have invested in Krugerrands or the Bolivar or another currency with the hopes that it would go up? What happens when that day comes when you need to cash in so that you can regain back your investment, yet the price has not increased in value as you had hoped? In fact, what if it has gone down and now you will lose much of the monies you invested?

What if a person who is depressed feels hopeless? Would that mean they could not be saved from their depression because they had no hope that they will get better? No. It means they do not have the tools or coping skills to accept what is. They have no hope that anything will improve, which is true. Maybe life will improve, maybe not.

You might think this all sounds hopeless. Or you may think, *So what if I am disappointed? I can handle it. It is just a feeling. So what if I lose money to try and make money? Isn't that what risk is all about?*

I used to think that one of my goals as a therapist was to provide hope for a client who comes in with depressed mood and a flat affect, as one criterion for depression may be hopelessness. I never really knew how to offer that hope other than the promise from me that one might improve. Early on in my training, I might have said, "I'm here to give you hope that you will get better."

Yet, I know now that depression—whether it is situational, has a genetic base, is caused from past abuse or from an illness such as heart disease or cancer, or whether it is accompanied by anxiety—is a disorder that can be treated by offering other methods to heal. Healing does not occur with the superficial and off-putting, "I hope you will find hope to get out of this hopeless place."

Did you know there were three saints called Faith, Hope and Charity? The only saints I knew were the nuns at a Catholic elementary school I attended. At least, they were *like* saints, cloaked in black robes and stoicism.

There was no hope in this Catholic school for me, only fear. During weekly Friday mass, priests would swing incense burners, no peppermints, nor meaningless nouns. (Remember the old Strawberry Alarm Clock song, *Incense and Peppermints?*) The scent of frankincense would stick in my nose hairs and I would become faint. I guess you could say I *hoped* for a way out of that weekly ritual, yet since the entire school had to grace the priests with our presence, it was wasted thought.

I chose this quote by Seneca for the meat of it—his brilliance at how happiness is to enjoy the present, without anxious dependence on the future. We don't need to look for an expectation of what may occur sometime near or far. Not anymore. Not in this second stage of life. We just need to find a way to be. Here. Now. That place of being here now and no place else is where we will find our peace.

That expectation of something other than *what is* sets us up for disappointments, sadness, grief, or a number of other avoidable emotions. It is okay to desire future rewards of some kind, but it is important to accept that they may or may not ever occur. We can allow ourselves those thoughts, and then let them just as quickly move on through our mind. If we get stuck in that place of wishing, hoping, or expecting a desire to come to fruition, we lose sight of the only place we can find joy, the here and now.

Are you thinking that without hope, you are giving up? Actually, it is just the opposite. It means you are giving in, to a place of acceptance of what is. You may not be okay with that state of mind that you are in, but there you are, in it nonetheless.

Suffering is necessary, hope is not. Hope for a way out is futile. Hope is not an action word, more a thought of what might be, of what the future *may* hold. The future holds what it holds.

We suffer because we feel. We experience life through our emotions and our physical bodies. An illness such as a cancer, diabetes, heart disease, lung problems, auto immune diseases, or an accident can cause physical pain and suffering. Hearing of another's diagnosis may cause suffering and emotional pain. A phobia or fear of something that will or might happen can cause us great suffering.

And sometimes the hope that our lives need to be different than they are can cause us suffering, that needless suffering that comes with wishful thinking.

THE HOPE OF PERFECTION

"If the world was perfect, it wouldn't be." —Yogi Berra

At this stage of life, extremes are not helpful and often destructive. They set you up to see your life as either one way or another. If you are a black-or-white person and believe there is a right vs. wrong answer to any of life's problems you may be a perfectionist. Perfectionism is a real affliction, an anxiety that can prevent you from feeling any joy in your life. If you have a need for everything in your life to be perfect, when it isn't, because of course nothing *is* perfect, you may feel like a failure and see yourself as less than—less than worthy. That less-than comparative analysis can lead to those thoughts of *I'm worthless and inadequate.*

If you need things to be perfect, you typically stay in a place of high expectations for yourself and the hope that you can fulfill them. Or you may have high expectations of your child, your spouse, a partner, parent or friend. Either way, those expectations and that hope can take you out of the moment and into the future which only the psychics amongst us can predict, or not.

Willis Weigand, an Associate Professor at Southwestern University in Georgetown, Texas, says that in his Introduction to General Chemistry Lab he has learned to offer his first-time students this mantra: "If you are a perfectionist, this laboratory will drive you nuts! No lab experiment works perfectly, so just do your best and keep going." Lab work is for performing experiments and a test may create or find something even more exciting than one had hoped.

More of my clients than not have a perfectionist view of their lives. A client, whom I will call Nancy, came in with high expectations of her spouse, which he was having trouble meeting: "I want my retired husband to find more things to do with himself. I wish he would want to travel more, keep the house clean, and go play cards with friends. Why can't he be more like Fred, Sally's husband? He helps her clean around the house and does it just like she wants. I'm hoping this new church will change him."

Nancy's husband often did help around the house but it wasn't good enough for her. He also had hobbies, they just were not ones of which she approved. She didn't feel that what *she* did was ever good enough, and she put these unrelenting demands on her husband as well. Her own inability to do things perfectly often made Nancy anxious. Even when she realized that all this stemmed from her mother's unrelenting high expectations towards her, Nancy remained paralyzed with anxiety and fears.

I asked Nancy to write about her mother's expectations of her and what that was like for her. She was afraid of the emotions that might come up; it scared her to get just words away from the suffering her thoughts held over her.

Yet, she did. In a relatively short amount of time, she was able to consider there were more than her ways to clean a house or live a retirement. She gained insight into how she felt about herself for not being perfect, and that she no longer needed to have everything in order to feel good about being human. She let up on her husband, and found more peacefulness in the new middle ground she allowed herself.

During my childhood, my own hope for the perfect family was based on prayer and the supernatural. I lived in a place of hope because to live in a household with arguments and fighting was worse than to be somewhere in my head hoping for a better future. And there was a nifty toy that helped me along with my inner fantasies.

Remember the Magic Eight Ball? That psychic black ball that had twenty answers to whatever questions your little heart desired? Back in the 50's, we kept one in our kitchen; that ball kept me occupied. I might ask a question like, "Will we be staying here in this house or moving to another?" or,

"Will Dad come home for dinner tonight or stay out until late like he often does?"

There were ten possible positive outcome responses. "It is certain," "You may rely on it," or "As I see it, Yes," were a few. If I ask the eight ball whether or not we will move, and it says, "You may rely on it," and then we move, well how do I know if it is prayer or the eight ball that caused it?

After a while, it didn't matter. The prayer that I learned to utilize when fear crept into my child's mind couldn't hold my attention like the eight ball could. I wondered if those nuns at my elementary school knew of this supernatural delight as an added component to prayer.

That small orb of black plastic, along with candy and sweets, was my childhood addiction. I might ask it a question and if one of the five indefinite answers like "Reply hazy, try again" or "Better not tell you now" came up, I would run upstairs, wait an interminable few minutes, run back down and ask again. Eventually, I was up and down the stairs, huffing and puffing, waiting for my next eight ball fix.

Hope is at the top rung of a ladder of our expectations, the upstairs of our childhood homes. It sets us up for failure, hurt, disappointment, immobilization, or the pursuit of perfection that doesn't exist. Besides taking us out of the present moment, the only place we can find joy, or peace, it prevents us from feeling what we are feeling. We need to feel *whatever* it is we are feeling.

THE ONLY WAY OUT IS THROUGH

When we experience the feelings of the moment, feel and acknowledge the pain and suffering, then we can pass through it, not get stuck in it, and move beyond it to the joy that can come from it.

The final conclusion at the end of the movie *Patton* was George C. Scott walking his dog with a voiceover saying how "All glory is fleeting." It was such a powerful conclusion to this war movie, because it was true. Like glory, feelings are fleeting. An emotion rarely lasts for long, if we allow ourselves to experience it. We may think that the way to rid ourselves of feeling pain, anxiety and suffering is to hope for something better. Again, that just takes us out of the moment. The only way to stop the pain and suffering that you may still be feeling is to feel it.

NO HOPE, NO WORRIES, NO JUDGMENT

So, how do you get away from what you wish you could feel or happen and be content with where you are? How do you stop hoping things will be different in your life?

Mindfulness is the key. Mindfulness is the quality or state of being conscious or aware of something. It is a mental state that is acquired when you focus your awareness on the present moment. As you come to acknowledge and accept what you are feeling, thinking, or sensing in your body, you are *okay* with this. You just are. Okay. With.This. It is happening and you are aware of it happening. No judgment.

So how do we *be* in the present moment? What does it mean to *be in the present?* Being in the present moment means to be aware of your surroundings. It is not thinking about the past, or the future, or where you have to be in an hour. It is taking stock of what you are doing right now.

Let's say your alarm goes off at seven a.m., you get out of bed, have some coffee, get in the shower, and while in the shower you are thinking of the list of all that you have to do that day. You realize you have been in there for some time so you get out, start to dry off and realize you haven't shaved your legs, or even washed your hair, though your hair is wet. In fact, you don't remember whether you washed down there or not. What were you doing in that shower? You know you were in there and the soap is wet, but you get back in just to make sure you got clean enough.

Back in the shower, you decide to stop thinking about the rest of the day, because it is a bit scary that you don't remember if you completed your routine. *Gosh, I hope it's not early-onset, or at my age, on-time Alzheimer's.* Instead, this time you just enjoy the moment, the water running down your face, watching the soap bubble up on your arms and legs, feeling the pressure as you scrub between your toes, listening to the water hit the tub as it rushes off your body.

This time you were in the moment. Without your mind preoccupied with that list of things to do, you could find joy and pleasure in those few minutes of starting your day. You didn't have to *hope* you had a good day, because your day started out that way. No hope, no worry, just enjoyment of being right where you were.

Now let's look at the non-judgmental aspect of being mindful and in the moment. Let's say that you are eating what you think is a sweet cherry but after that first bite you taste a sour flavor, wince at the tartness and your mouth waters. You swallow and you notice what you are experiencing, the sourness of the cherry. You do this without judging whether the cherry is good or bad. It is just tart and sour. It just is what it is.

Is your mouth watering right now? If so, you just experienced an in-the-moment vicarious thrill, and you didn't have to wish yourself there. It just happened. You were in the present moment.

MEDITATION AND ITS BENEFITS

Meditation is one of the best ways to learn how to be in the moment. Meditation is a practice of concentrated focus upon the breath, a sound, a word or mantra in order to increase the awareness of the present moment. It can promote relaxation, reduce stress levels and enhance personal and spiritual growth. It is considered one of the better methods of reducing panic disorder, generalized anxiety disorder and physical pain.

There are several types of meditation techniques: movement, mindful and concentration. For our purposes, I want to focus on the Mindfulness Meditation technique. In mindful meditation, you notice your thoughts and feelings and allow yourself to have them. Accept whatever thoughts come up while practicing a detachment from them by not having a judgment of whether they are good or bad.

If you are sitting in a chair, your feet should be touching the ground, with hands in your lap or on your knees. You may want to sit in a Lotus position on the floor, cross-legged with each foot placed on the opposing thigh. It is important to relax your body to a place where there is no tension or pain, if possible. If you do notice any tension or pain, no need to judge it, just allow it to be. Or you can move around a bit to see if you can release any tension that may form in one part of your body.

The purpose is to allow any thoughts to come in, and not to critique them. If you are feeling anxious and worry that you will be unable to sit for twenty minutes with all your negative thoughts about yourself, start with five minutes.

However, sitting quietly and not feeling anxious can be hard to do, especially if you are worried about the future or live in a state of fear. To sit in a quiet place for even five minutes when your mind is filled with worry about the past or the future can be difficult, to say the least.

Fifteen years ago, I attended a seminar presented by Ron Siegel, PsyD, and Psychology faculty member at Harvard Medical School. He offered a Mindfulness Workshop for therapists in how to use these techniques in our practice. A colleague asked me to join her, and while I was up for learning new techniques, I was not up for experiencing any mediation for myself.

My own therapist, that very wise man, had told me about it; it was all the rage and had been since TM, or Transcendental Meditation, had hit the states in the 60's, our decade of transformation. I had never tried it during that time so now, in my forties, when I did sit still with my thoughts and try to calm them, it was like putting lighter fluid on lit charcoal. I had *hoped* we would not have to experience this technique during the workshop; that hope kept me in a state of anxiety up until that dreaded day.

Ron showed some slides of how helpful mediation is for calming the mind and keeping us in the moment. *Nice slides,* I thought. *Maybe I will ask him where he gets them, or, even better, I'll just take notes so I can get all this information out to my clients.* It was supposed to be a very useful technique and I was excited to learn from one of the best clinicians in our field.

"Now," Ron said in a mildly hypnotic tone intended to put us at ease, "I want to take you through a twenty-minute meditation. I will lead you through it for a minute or two, and then you will go there yourselves and be in the moment. Be still while you focus on your breathing. Allow any thoughts to move through you. You do not have to judge them; just allow them to move through your consciousness. Remember we will be in this state for twenty minutes. Everyone close their eyes."

Twenty minutes? Holy lifetime, Batman.

What I heard was, "The guillotine will slice right through your neck. It will happen so fast you won't notice any bleeding, any negative thoughts, just peaceful loss of life. And now we begin our death wish."

My heart pounded, my thoughts raced, sweat began to bead on my face; I was in full panic mode. I had wished, yet again that place of wishful thinking, that there really was a guillotine over my head and that he would quickly release the blade. Fast. Now. In-the-moment.

The last place I wanted to be was in a room with a hundred people all with our eyes closed and me with my thoughts. Those awful, anxious, negative thoughts and fears that spoke to me in a way no one ever had.

You can't do this, you'll fail and then you will go running from the room, arms over your head, screaming like a maniac. And even though I have never seen a maniac, I will be the first to have others see me this way and I will make a fool out of myself, my maniacal self, and be so embarrassed and ashamed that I will have to run away from here, where I will end up who knows but it will be very, very far from here, from all these thoughts in my head and all those thoughts everyone will have about me and... No. I. Can't. Do. This.

I didn't want to be in this room with all those meditators, nor did I wish, want or care to be alone outside this room with my thoughts. *How do I get out of this? What do I do? Should I just get up and go to the bathroom and wait until it is all over? Oh, this is awful.*

I am awful. I can't even sit with my eyes closed for twenty minutes for God's sake. What is wrong with me? Everyone else is able to do this.

I hope and pray this is over soon. I wish I had the Magic Eight Ball here to see how much longer I may have to endure this.

I am such a fool! What kind of fool am I? Who never falls in love...it seems that I'm the only............Anthony Newley sang that, oh, Sammy Davis, Jr. did too. I like him........................ Oh, my, I wonder how many minutes it has been since this started. I'll just squint and see if Ron is doing this along with us. Maybe there is a big enough clock in here that I can see how many more minutes we have.........I can do this, I can do this, I can do this...............

"Okay, everyone. You can start moving around in your chairs. Start coming back into the room. And when you are ready, open your eyes."

Where has everyone else been? I've been here the whole excruciating time. There was no way I was going to let myself have an out-of-body experience and go running through the room like some fool about whom Anthony Newley sang.

Ron asked for comments on what the experience was like.

"It was a wonderfully peaceful and calm experience. It took me a while to just let my thoughts go, but after a while, I almost got sleepy," one woman remarked.

Sleepy? How in the world do you get sleepy? I haven't been this anxious since, well, since yesterday when I had to give that presentation.

It was time to speak up.

"Could you please tell me how long it takes before the anxiety goes away?" I mustered up the courage to ask. I realized I was almost angry—with myself, I presumed.

"Yes, some people get anxious but it will go away in time."

"Some people get anxious." I was one of those people, an anxiety-ridden wishful thinker who couldn't take twenty minutes to find peace of mind.

Surprisingly, having to be in a group of people all experiencing this at the same time for twenty minutes really did help break my fears. After this episode, I didn't go back to it for over a year. When I finally did, it took me many sessions of five minutes each to break the fear and anxiety that this method brought up in me. Once I managed five minutes, I could easily last for twenty. The good thing about meditation is that it is cumulative. The benefits of sitting with your mind in a non-judgmental way can, over time, lessen any negative self-talk and any anxiety about the future.

Since this episode where I was forced, or *encouraged*, to sit with my fears, negative self-talk, horrific worry about what I might do or not be able to do, and many more self-imposed minutes of meditation, the anxiety has left the building, my building.

Now I can sit, and be still, alone with my thoughts. There is no angst, no negativity, no thoughts about future worries or fears, or that I will go crazy, blurt out something foolish or need to run from the room.

You can become okay with yourself and you can really sit, and *be*.

At times, I still think about future events when I am meditating, or what I need to get at the grocery store, or what I will wear to some dinner engagement, but it is not painful. It is peaceful. It is me being with myself and with whatever comes up in that moment.

I came to realize, after my mother died, that hope exists only in our minds and takes us out of the present. For two years I hoped for something different, to feel anything other than grief, to be anyplace than with my sad and lonely thoughts and feelings. I even concocted ways for her to come back.

She was a pilot during the war, one of just 1,830 women chosen to fly for the Air Corps in WWII. She and the other female pilots ferried bombers and pursuit planes from one end of the country to the other, preparing those planes for the male pilots to take them overseas. My father was her instruments rating pilot and signed off for her to fly in turbulent weather. That was how they met.

So, my thought was that she was invincible. While I knew she wasn't, maybe it was possible, I had hoped, for her to fly back down to earth from wherever she was and come back in the flesh one day. Maybe she had some pilot training we weren't aware of that allowed her to fly through several ozone layers; maybe Dad had taught her powers to come back after death and combined with all the new technology, she would manage to zoom in at the speed of light through the atmosphere and parachute into her home.

Along with the hope that some miracle might occur, I also wanted to be anywhere than with the sorrow and grief of losing her, and the misery I felt in missing her. When I was able to let go of the hope that things would change and be different, only then could I experience gratitude for having had my mother in my life, and experience the joy, peace of mind and comfort I sought.

If happiness is not the absence of pain, conflict, suffering, or anxiety, then you can still be in the moment, find joy, peace and delight, without hope being your lifeline.

ACTION PLAN

1. Identify for yourself every time you use the word hope. It might be in your thoughts. Or you may find that you often use it as part of your language. "I hope I get this job because I

don't know what I will do if not." "I hope my daughter finally sees the light and dumps that useless boyfriend," or "I hope my son gets a job soon or else he might live with us forever."

2. What do these types of thoughts do for you? How do they make you feel? Do they stop you in your tracks and make you feel useless? Or do they make you feel like you are doing something about a problem? How does using the concept of hope serve you? Whom do you know that uses the term "hope" a lot? A pastor, a family member, you?

3. Each time you find yourself thinking *hopefully* about a problem in your life, think instead, *What can I do about this?* There might be an action you can take to make yourself feel better or move you forward, closer to a solution to some problem.

4. Seneca was a Stoic philosopher. To be stoic implies a lack of vulnerability and an imposing façade to the outside world. This characteristic may flourish in the corporate world. This trait may even bring about the greed and avarice we see today in the financial system. What do you think about this? Do you see stoicism as a positive trait? Or see yourself as stoic? If so, who in your family was like that? How does it serve you? How does it hinder you? How are you different now than you were in the first stage of life? What may you have hoped for that didn't happen, yet something even better did?

5. Do you see yourself as a perfectionist? If so, how so? How has it been helpful to have those perfectionist traits? How has it been destructive?

6

FORGIVENESS, FUGGEDDABOUTIT

"Forgiveness is not an occasional act, it is a constant attitude."

Martin Luther King, Jr.

Forgiveness is difficult. It may be the hardest act for us humans to grasp. It just doesn't add up with our feelings about fairness, the nature of how we view justice, equality and righteousness. We hold grudges and spout epithets to those who have wronged us. It is the natural essence of life; "Do onto others what they have done onto us" may be more of a motto we have instead of the actual biblical scripture of "Do unto others what you would have them do unto you."

Not forgiving by harboring any past hurts or resentment can cause us great anxiety. If we are ever to get beyond our anxiety and any pain and suffering, forgiving is the key to a more joyful place. It is the letting go of the need to get revenge and releasing negative thoughts of resentment and bitterness towards someone who betrayed our trust, boundaries, or kind nature.

How in the world do we do that?

During the 1800's, the way disagreements were settled may have been to seek revenge at any cost, including taking another's life. The long-standing feud between the two families, the Hatfields and the McCoys, who lived across the Tug Fork River from each other, one family in Kentucky, the other in West Virginia, was settled that way. They fought over land, different Civil War allegiances, and had revenge killings when one family member became angry with a member of the other family.

I remember watching a video in my undergraduate Anthropology class about a tribe and their style of retribution. When one member of an Aboriginal tribe was killed for any reason, the other tribe would retreat, form a plan for a front line assault and the following day move forward and kill one member of the opposing tribe. They didn't perform a massacre or try to kill all the members of that clan; rather it was an eye for an eye, tooth for a tooth, one man for one man, pure and simple justice in a pure and simple culture.

But our twenty-first-century society is not simple. We don't have an eye for an eye justice. We can't morally or legally respond in kind if another life is taken. It just doesn't work in our more complex civilization.

Yet, this eye for an eye justice is often how we think of fairness. If someone does something to us, then our first inclination is to do something back to them at the same level of the one on which they hurt us. If your friend stabs you in the back with words, well then, stab her back with your own vicious words. If a spouse hurt you with an affair, you may not have an affair on him or her to get back at them, yet you may withhold love, affection, sex, kindness, for as long as you choose to make them pay for their behavior.

We deal with injustice by trying to hurt another, which can cause us to suffer emotionally and or physically when we hold on to some hurt of which we can't let go. We can become overwrought with anxiety, angst and anger.

In this second stage of life, you may find yourself keeping score of all the horrific deeds perpetrated upon you. You may be holding onto betrayal by a spouse, or an ex-spouse. You may have been abused as a child, verbally, emotionally, physically or even sexually. A parent may have neglected your needs and now you seek love, approval and acceptance from without, instead of within.

You might also keep track of the petty slights perpetrated upon you; someone may have left you off their wedding list, invited other neighbors to dinner without you, or neglected to send a birthday card.

How do we forgive someone who has betrayed our trust, our boundaries, and our friendship? Is it possible to forgive someone for something egregious they have done? What makes it so important to do so?

You may wonder, *Why can't I continue to be angry towards the husband who abused me or the war that made me kill? Don't they deserve to be banned from my forgiving them forever? And if I forgive, how will they get theirs? How can they do this to me and get away with it? This isn't fair.*

YOU CAN BE ANGRY, JUST KNOW THAT WHAT HAPPENED IS NOT FAIR

As far as being angry about any deed perpetrated upon you, of course you can be angry. Anger is a response to a hurt, or a way to express a fear that something might happen or has happened despite your fear. Anger says: "You did something that you shouldn't have done. I didn't like it that you moved over into my lane and now are going under the speed limit.

You could cause an accident by going too slow. I followed the rules. You should, too. It's not fair. I don't like it and I am angry about it. I could have been hurt."

Anger speaks loudly, shouting its opinion at the unfairness of it all. "My brother became ill after we both were bitten by the same spider. It should have been me. It's not fair."

Anger can eat you up inside and cause you pain and suffering if you don't let it go. Anger turns into resentment over time, keeps you in the past and can make you physically sick with worry over how to get back at some injustice.

There was a time when the psychotherapy community used to believe that when you are angry, you should get in your car and bang your fists on the dashboard while screaming at the top of your lungs. And all of this while driving!

We know better now. We know that anger begets more anger, which can beget violence. It's not healthy nor is it helpful to us or the other person towards whom we may inflict this anger. Acknowledging your anger is healthy; acting it out is not.

We also know that life is not fair. There are no assurances that if I do this, you will do that and we will both keep our promises. We can not be assured through a gentleman's handshake, a written contract, a blood brother's or sister's promise, a verbal assurance, a swear of loyalty, or even a miracle, that something might not happen to reverse the guarantee that never really was.

FORGIVE ME

"Forgiveness says you are given another chance to make a new beginning." Desmond Tutu

What is forgiveness, anyway, and what does it have to do with this book on anxiety in the second half of life? Does it matter if I can forgive or not? Can't I still find joy in my life without doing that?

To be able to forgive is to no longer feel anger towards someone, or to be able to stop blaming someone for something they did. Or to stop being angry with yourself for something you did. If you are still holding on to old hurts, you are living in the past. Without forgiveness, anxiety may continue to flourish.

Forgiveness is also described as the intentional and voluntary process by which you undergo a change in feelings and attitude for an offense that was done to you. It is letting go of negative emotions like vengefulness. It may include an ability to actually wish an offender well.

If someone has *asked* for forgiveness for tragic behavior, then it would be more understandable that you might get to a place to wish them well. But it would be awfully hard to do so if they have not apologized for their behavior. And yet, it is possible.

However, these are just definitions. They don't tell you how to forgive.

You can learn what forgiveness is by looking at the people who seem to have been able to live forgiveness: the acceptance of Buddha, the words of Nelson Mandela, the kindness of Mother Teresa, and the turn-the-other-cheek lessons of Jesus.

Nelson Mandela was imprisoned for twenty-seven years by the South African apartheid government for leading a campaign to overthrow their racist policies. He was quoted as saying, "As I walked out the door toward the gate that would lead to my freedom, I knew if I didn't leave my bitterness and hatred behind, I'd still be in prison."

If anyone had a right to be bitter, resentful and angry, it would be Nelson Mandela for the time he spent in prison for standing up for the rights and abuses of other black South Africans. Instead, he made the choice to let go of his anger and resentment; he made an active decision to do so.

"Not forgiving is like drinking rat poison and waiting for the rat to die." Anne Lamott.

Still, you may say, "But these are exceptional human beings. Sure, they may be able to forgive but how can I without the grace, the heart, the intellect, or the ability to be kind to that guy that wronged me the way these extraordinary exceptions have let something go?"

Well, the solution is in the problem. The problem and the solution is that you are human, too. You deserve the same benefits that suit any other human being. For if one can do this very difficult work of forgiveness, you can also. You must believe that. And that which you seek will occur. What will occur in the place of the hurt and resentment will be gratitude for the life you do have, and the joy that comes with that appreciation.

To forgive or not to forgive. That is one question.

The other question is whether we need to *forget* what the other person did to us as we grant them forgiveness. Or not.

A way we feign forgiveness is with the tagline: "But I will never forget!"

Are you holding these words as a banner of your truth so you can appear to forgive, but secretly never let go of a grudge? As though forgiving but not forgetting the hurt is the way to lessen the pain, excuse your trespasser and move on with your life.

To say "I will forgive but not forget" is really no different than holding on to some vestige of the past so that we can continue to hold the sword of Damocles over someone's head that may have violated our boundaries. We think that will grant us deliverance from suffering.

That choice to forgive but not forget continues to damage our soul and psyche which may also seep into our mental state and corrode our physical one. It does not lessen our anxiety or allow us to find joy and sustain peace in our lives.

Of course that doesn't mean we must forget something that happened. I am not an advocate of any treatment that makes you forget anything or of trying to erase your mind of some unwanted memory. If you had a traumatic memory, it is not about forgetting it; it is about finding a new narrative, a new perspective of what it meant, what it means to you now, and how to live with any lessons that may be there for the taking.

What would self-forgiveness look like in all of these instances? How do we forgive ourselves for past regrets? What makes it important to do so?

When people say they have forgiven themselves for an act about which they feel badly, they are making an active choice to acknowledge the wrongdoing and acknowledge any participating role in their actions. They then can let go of the negative thoughts over this mistake, error, blunder, or sin, depending on how they view their deeds.

It can be a difficult task to let ourselves off the hook for a misdeed. If you tend to worry or obsess about what you may have done to harm someone, or what you perceive might have been harmful, it can take a lifetime to be able to soulfully hug ourselves and say, "I forgive me."

During an Eye Movement Desensitization and Reprocessing (EMDR) workshop, a presenter told us how he helps veterans with trauma forgive themselves. He has them think of what they did on a balance scale and put all the misdeeds on one side. Then he has them think about the ways they can add to their lives and the lives of others through acts of kindness or generosity of spirit to create a balance on the scale to equal what they believed they did wrong.

Forgiving ourselves is an extremely important component of ever being able to forgive someone else whom has trespassed against us. If we can't forgive ourselves for our participation or role in an event, how can we ever experience the letting go from a perpetrator?

SHAME ON ME

If you were abused, physically or sexually, you may ask yourself, "Could I have stopped it? Why did I allow it to happen? I could have run from the room, hit back, maimed my abuser, kicked, struggled and fought until I got away. Couldn't I have? Why didn't I?"

Not forgiving ourselves for whatever responsibility we believe we have in a hurtful or traumatic act just adds to the shame of it all. Any traumatic event can bring about self-shame from which we need to heal. When we behave or act in some way we regret, we may feel embarrassed for our behavior. We may feel hurt, sad, or guilty for our bad behavior.

But if something happens to us that we regret, or we participate in an act we lament and wish we had not done, when we then think of ourselves as *bad*, that is shame.

Shame sticks to us like glue. It is secretive, hidden, invisible yet burdensome. It covers us with its heavy coating. When our hidden shame comes into public or external view, or at least when we allow ourselves to be vulnerable and accept it, that is how we will get rid of it. It is the denial, the hiding of what happened to us, that secret we hold, those vulnerabilities that keep us in that place of shame that can create worry and anxiety of being found out.

Once you have faced your own hidden or denied self, there is not much more to be anxious about because there is no fear of exposure, to yourself or to others.

The first time I ever felt the shame another person was experiencing was when I worked in an Atlanta psychiatric hospital. I had felt my own shame many times from past experiences yet never another person's humiliation until this one day.

A patient assigned to another social worker sat on the windowsill of the large open reception area in the group wing of the hospital. As he waited for his social worker to be available, he looked troubled. I wanted to connect with him to see if he wanted to talk.

Head hung low, he stared at the floor. I asked what was wrong. He quickly looked away. I sat in a chair and waited. When I asked him what brought him to the hospital, he shook his head again. I lingered nearby until he was ready.

He told me he was there for an addiction problem. Cocaine. He said that he would do anything for that drug. Anything. Like sex. I nodded and listened as he began to shake his head some more, put his hand up to his face and whisper, "I had sex with another man. More than once. All for cocaine." He began to sob.

He didn't say much more. His shame was palpable. I felt it for him. Shame had swallowed him whole, and it wasn't until he spit it out that he could start to heal. But it would take time.

This connection to forgiving himself was more complicated than if some act was done to him. It was his participation in a disgraceful deed that hurt his psyche and his soul. Yet, it is the self-forgiveness that will allow one to be healed no matter how or what happened.

"Forgiveness is giving up all hope of having had a better past." Anne Lamott

If you experienced abuse by a family member or an acquaintance, or by someone you did not know, you may feel shame. The shame may be about having such a horrid experience occur to you, it may be that your family member did this in a very loving manner, it may be that you might have enjoyed a part of it, or felt loved by this person.

Many sexual abusers were abused themselves and saw this as an act of love and learned that this was how you show love, horrendous and convoluted as it may be to think about, to one's own children. One day during a group therapy session, a group member began to share about how he would be leaving the hospital and going on to jail for sexually abusing his young sons. He told the group that his father too had abused him, but that as he grew up, he learned to see it as a very loving act. It was familiar to him. He had never processed what occurred to him as a child, so he continued to fondle his own children.

As I looked around at the other group members, I saw in them what I tried to ensure didn't happen to me. The entire group reacted with jaws dropped and a grimace, another one of those times where there were no words. This was not a topic that needed to be shared in a group setting. My goal was to ensure that this member did not further traumatize the others in the room.

Since those almost unfathomable words we heard, I have heard other men and women state the same thing, that they felt loved when they were touched by a family member, often a parent. Still they feel ashamed as they learn to deal with the damaging effects of wounds inflicted by an elder who was supposed to protect them. Sexual abuse, and even physical abuse, while very damaging to the psyche and body, can often be forgiven more easily than neglect. Neglect, or not having attention paid to you from a parent, can be more painful for someone to reconcile than any other form of abuse.

WHY ME?

While you may feel a need to explore why something happened to you, it can be a fruitless and endless quest. When you ask "why," you are looking for answers, and answers are about cause and effect. There may be numerous factors to explain why something happens to us. Trying to dig to the actual cause of an event can be as fruitless as being stoned in the 60's or 70's trying to figure out how we came to exist. We will never know the answer.

Most likely many factors are in play: genetic, environmental, psychological, and biological. Yet the exact reasons or motives as to why may never be found. You could spend a lifetime trying to answer a "why" question. And your lifetime will be spent in an anxious conundrum of worry whether you are right or not.

It is more important to learn how you now view a trauma that happened to you, and what you make of it. It is more important to ask, "How can I get past this? What do I need to do to heal? What sense can I make of this?" These are questions in which you will find meaning and ways to forgive yourself, and to heal from any past trauma so that you can be in the moment, the only place you will find any peace of mind.

In couples therapy, one aspect of healing that can take place for both spouses is when one spouse hears how another was brought up. The past issues that your partner went through are crucial in learning how to forgive an affair or an injustice. Often a person has seen the ongoing acceptance of affairs or other wrongs from some family member in their past. It becomes unconsciously, or even consciously, accept-able.

It is not that a spouse has not had their needs met by their partner that they choose an affair. It is because somehow, they see that as an acceptable thing to do.

With any trauma there is shame, and with any shame there may be trauma. So, if trauma occurs, you will feel shame, thus the importance of learning to forgive yourself for any-thing you are holding onto of which you need to let go.

It is vital to work on yourself and any anxieties that may come up related to your own transgressions or those of some-one with whom you are in a relationship. Work on yourself, so that you can be the best you can be for yourself, your part-ner and the community. Remember that this is your journey in life.

GRACE: DOES IT HAVE TO FALL INTO YOUR LAPTOP?

One of the most beautiful descriptions about grace is best said in yet another quote by Anne Lamott: *"I do not under-stand the mystery of grace—only that it meets us where we are and does not leave us where it found us."*

If you are a spiritual person and believe in a higher power, you may believe that your ability to forgive a trespass was about grace; that somehow, out of the blue, you were given a moment of understanding that you no longer had to hold on to some transgression done to you, or that you committed. If forgiveness or acceptance seems to come out of nowhere or fall into your lap, that may be seen as grace. If that occurs, that can be a beautiful thing.

Richard Rohr, a Franciscan priest in New Mexico and founder of the Center for Action and Contemplation in Al-buquerque, writes in his book, *Falling Upward*, "If you have forgiven yourself for being imperfect and falling, you can now do it for just about everybody else."

If grace does not seem to fall into your lap, you can do the work to heal on your own. That work means to see forgiveness not as a momentary action, but a lifelong way of perceiving an event, the world even. If you can change your attitude about something that happened to you, you can find the freedom from anxiety that comes with not being able to forgive, and the joy that can fill your heart instead.

ACTION PLAN

1. What are you holding onto of which you need to let go and for which you need to forgive yourself? A thought, a trespass, maybe even a relationship?

2. What has someone done to you or to a loved one for which you want to forgive them? Have you ever told anyone about this? Maybe a therapist, a spouse, a trusted friend, a pastor? Was it helpful to do so? If you have not shared this event(s), what has kept you from telling your story?

3. Have you ever said, "I can forgive but not forget?" What do you think about that statement now? Is it keeping you from letting go? Be honest with yourself

4. How has shame manifested itself in your life? Have you experienced your own shame? Have you ever noticed how you shame another with your words or actions? Where do you think your shame comes from? Journal on this.You

can keep the writing or tear it up. You can even burn it. If you do, let your shame and anxieties burn with it into ashes.

5. Have you ever experienced grace? In what way? What was that experience like for you?

7

IF THE SPIRIT MOVES YOU, MOVE WITH IT

"According to Vedanta, there are only two symptoms of enlightenment, just two indications that a transformation is taking place within you toward a higher consciousness. The first symptom is that you stop worrying. Things don't bother you anymore. You become light-hearted and full of joy. The second symptom is that you encounter more and more meaningful coincidences in your life, more and more synchronicities. And this accelerates to the point where you actually experience the miraculous."

Deepak Chopra, Synchrodestiny: Harnessing the Infinite Power of Coincidence to Create Miracles

Fundamentally, there are two questions you may have asked yourself, which in the very large schema of things can produce a multitude of anxious thoughts. The first question is our most primary wonderment of all for which there are no answers. As early as the age of reason, we begin to wonder about the beginnings of life on Earth. How did we come to be on this planet? What are the origins of the universe?

While we may still wonder about this, how we came to be here is more of a first stage of life pursuit. The other question we now may be asking ourselves in this second half of life is why we are here.

We wonder about our personal meaning, the small picture within the grander picture. How do we make a difference in life, what is our individual purpose and how do we live that purpose in a joyful, spirit-filled way? If we choose self-exploration, we can learn how to exercise our soul to find enjoyment, lessen our anxiety about what others might think of us, and rise above the hassles and worries of daily life.

If you attended Sunday school, parochial school, Vacation-Bible School, or went to church with your parents, you have been told the stories of the Bible, the Torah, or some other religious explanation for the origins to our journey here. It is right there in black or white. It is the word, the word of God. Despite the fact that the word has been written in words other than God's words and translated multiple times throughout history, these words are said to be God's words. The pure and simple truth; something that is neither pure nor simple.

Is God the answer to your anxious query of how we came to be? Or do you believe in the Big Bang, a theory that states that the universe's dense hot state exploded into what we now know as the universe, as the creation point of the world? Maybe you accept Evolution theory as Darwin states? Did we develop over billions of years from both living and non-living organisms and genetically mutate into edibles, inedibles, and the human species?

Were Greek philosophers like Anaximander, who lived 500 years Before Christ, and who postulated the development of life from non-life and the evolutionary descent of man from animal, *right?*

Carl Sagan, the astronomer and astrophysicist who popularized science and life beyond the Cosmos, said that Anaximander produced one of the first recorded scientific experiments. One of Anaximander's ideas was that humans came from the mouths of big fish that protected us from the Earth's climate because we could not survive in the open air until we had been almost fully formed.

Sounds like a fish story to me. *And the fish was thiiiiiiiiiis big!*

It is easy to see our struggle to answer this unanswerable wonder.

If you delve deeper into what it is that you believe, where does your "how" start? If you believe in God, how did God get here? Certainly for many religious folks, that is an absurd question, as they choose to believe, without questioning further, that God made the universe. God made God. God was first, always and forever more. Period. The Beginning. The End.

If you do believe in the Big Bang, or Evolution theory, how did that begin? Who, or what, lit that fuse? If it were not for our God, by God, than by whom or how?

No matter what or how you believe, every point of origin had to start somewhere. This is where a reasonable person may believe that both God and Evolution can coexist.

You can see all the unease that trying to figure out or understand the universe brings up. For it is this uncertainty about the origins of life that may keep us riddled with anxiety about the source of our existence.

"Silence is the language of God, all else is poor translation." – Rumi

We wonder about our lives; it is natural, and essential. For many people, religion serves them with answers to their queries, despite each religion having slightly different answers to the wonder of how we came to be, and what happens after we leave this life. Each religion has its answers to our evolution, how we are to live our lives during our time on Earth, and what happens after we die.

It is human nature to want answers to the uncertainties of life. Uncertainty breeds anxiety. Religion allows that *certainty* for some. It can be a comfort to believe that you have the map of life and the way to get there.

For others the dogmatic theories of religion are off-putting. Many children who attended parochial schools witnessed firsthand the hypocrisies and inflexible disciplines that may have created many of their anxieties that carried through to adulthood and made them question who is right and who has the answers.

During an elementary English class at that Catholic school I attended, a peer named Rosanna sat in the front row next to me. Rosanna was shy like myself and never raised her hand to answer questions. I noticed this, as I was of similar ilk. There were many rules in this Catholic school—one of which was there were certain times you went to the restroom; during class was not one of those times. In one particular grammar session, Sister Mary Lou asked the class a question and then looked around the room, focusing directly on her target, my friend and fellow nervous student, Rosanna Angst.

"Rosanna, what is the verb in this diagram?"

At that moment the room fell quiet. The students whose hands were raised dropped them abruptly. And then the worst-case scenario happened.

All you could hear was the trickling of urine that seeped from Rosanna's uniform off the wooden seat of her desk onto the linoleum floor. I looked over at my classmate who stared straight ahead while tears ran down her cheeks. I really don't remember what happened next because time stood still. The video replay in my mind stops as I fixate on Rosanna. I wondered if she was thinking what I would have been thinking right then.

What do I do now? Do I just get up from my seat and run from the room? Should I ask the teacher what to do? Will I ever be able to face this class again? What will happen when I get home? Will I have to endure a hand slap from my father for doing something so terrible in class? Or will my punishment be worse? Maybe the belt about which I had always heard. Would this awful deed warrant that penalty?

I do remember that Rosanna didn't come back to school for days and nothing was ever said about it. We were all left with an unknowing of what to expect of ourselves. *What really happened? Could that happen to me? What if it happened to me?*

How awful for her. No one ever told us to raise our hands to ask to use the restroom if needed during class to prevent a similar occurrence. What I do remember is that my worry that I might have to use the restroom during class affected me throughout my school career.

Looking back it seemed that while the nuns in that Catholic school were married to God, the one who had the answers to the Universe, they still had these inhumane rules that could bring up anxiety affecting us for the rest of our lives. I still wonder if my classmate ever got over the humiliation and shame of that incident.

For many, the dogmatic one-way answer is as anxiety-provoking as the not knowing. How can an all-knowing, all-loving God allow a seven-year-old girl to be so frightened and anxious that she would pee on herself? How are some of us saved if we believe the *right* way while others must burn in hell for not believing? How can people of certain religions be right while other religions are wrong? To circumvent this difficult to fathom dogma and the anxiety it can produce, some people don't believe in God.

"Faith is a knowledge within the heart, beyond the reach of proof." – Khalil Gibran

Others may choose to have faith, a belief in God, and at the same time have many questions and few, if any, answers. You may still believe in a higher power, you just aren't sure what will happen after we die. You may have faith that we all will be saved from Hell, if you believe in Hell at all, because we are a flawed human race. You might choose to believe in reincarnation, or a Heaven-type state of being, or of being reunited with loved ones. You may believe Heaven or Hell is right here on Earth and that nothing happens after we die. With your faith, you may still have lots more questions than answers, and you make choices that fill your soul instead of your need for someone else's truth.

In the 70's, when I was in my twenties, my mother owned and operated a health food store in Southern Florida. I would work with her in the summer during college breaks.

One day a tall, thin man came in interested in a book about how sugar was harmful and planned on buying it for his sister. He didn't look like he needed it for himself. I asked him if it was *Sugar Blues.* He said yes and asked how I knew that.

"Well, it's a pretty popular book and I've gotten acquainted with most of the books we stock."

"I didn't remember the name of the book I was looking for. I've been in a bit of a trance lately since getting back from India and studying the truths of life," he said.

"The truths of what?" I asked naively. Did he say "life?" I wondered if I was getting ready to find the answers to the questions I had not yet pondered.

"The truths of life as practiced in Buddhism. It is all you really need to know."

"Well, what are they?" I pleaded internally but asked with a false detachment.

"Oh, we can't share that. This is something one learns after spending time in meditation and prayer with spiritual leaders."

I remember how my insides felt mushy, like I was so close to the truth yet so far because this attractive young man was going to keep me from learning the meaning of life. Was this burning desire love, I wondered, or maybe this is what it feels like to be close to someone with the answers. It was a feeling that could go either way on the scale of love to hate and I was bordering on the less friendly side of the spectrum after his comment.

"Well, can you just tell me one, or give me a hint? I won't tell anyone else, I promise, really, and I mean that." I wasn't sure what I meant.

"These truths are very simple and available to all of us, though you must learn them for yourself in your own way," he finished.

At that young age my main thought was that he was cute. I even imagined that he seemed slightly interested in me. Maybe that was just the daze he was in from his flight back from India, or maybe he was giddy and filled with the Holy Spirit. Whatever the reason, my chance for answers was gone for now, and it was over between us.

Several weeks later, he came in again for another book. I was friendly, but kept my distance. My belief was that truth is meant to be shared, not something you keep to yourself. Even before I ever thought about graduate school in social work, I did have one strong view of his refusal to share any truths with me. Diagnosis: selfish.

When this exchange was later relayed to my mom, she said, "That guy is full of it. Do you think he would be coming in here if he knew the truth about life? Sue, that's a bunch of bunk." Then we laughed and got back to our unanswerable lives.

I was in the first half of my life at that time and wasn't on a quest for my truths. My focus was on how to keep my anxiety and negative thoughts at bay. That was enough of a challenge without considering the bigger picture of my life.

Though that episode made me think that real truth or answers really should be shared. If they were universally true, like the answer to life, or how we got here, simple or complex, could someone please put it on a billboard or post it on Facebook so the whole world, or at least so our Facebook friends, could see it?

Since no one has the answer down pat, the truth can only come from *within* you. This exploration of what is true for you is paramount to finding joy and peace. Exploring your beliefs and how you live according to those beliefs can be where you find your purpose and meaning.

Now, you may be more focused on: *Why am I here? What is my purpose for being here on earth What do I want to do with the time I have while on this earth?* These questions may still take a lifetime to answer yet are ones in which you will find comfort once you imagine your life's meaning and worth. Unless you value hedonism, you probably will find that the answer to these questions will have something to do with making a difference in the world, and making the world a better place.

Clients often come in to the therapy office at this stage looking for the meaning of life. They really are asking, "What is the meaning of *my* life? How can I contribute to the world? How can I make a difference?" We need to know what significance our life has for us. Not knowing can produce all kinds of anxieties, especially at this time of life. I think this is what

Erikson meant when he wrote about the importance of his psychosocial conflict of Generativity versus Stagnation.

When we are able to give back to society in some way, create and nurture something that will outlast us, then we can have a sense of making a difference in someone else's life, which in turn will make a difference in our life. This contribution to the whole is self-sustaining and feeds our soul. It creates that internal and external connection to the universe, your universe, and it can lessen any free-floating anxiety you have.

This is where spirituality comes in, as spirituality is about meaning—the meaning you place on the wonderment of life, the beauty of nature, the mix of awe and glorious splendor that exists around us and within us. Joy can exist in the spirit of the moment as you admire that magnificence of the universe of which you are a part.

Spirituality is a vague concept with many different meanings. If you see yourself as a spiritual person, being spiritual may mean you have had a personal transformation that is in some way a religious experience. It may mean you have an attachment or regard for things of the spirit more than you do towards material or worldly interests. It often includes religious feelings and beliefs, including a sense of peace, purpose, connection to others and the universe, and beliefs about the meaning of life.

Or it may resonate more as a subjective meaningful occurrence or joyful experience that comes from a personal psychological growth.

However you view spirituality, I want to use the sense of spirit as an internal, soulful pull that allows you to follow your heart. A heartfelt wisdom that tugs on you to have fun, dance, laugh, feel joy, sing, or cry. Whatever brings out the wonderment of you, the in-the-moment feel-it, experience-it, do-it, be-it spirit that you allow yourself to express without critical internal thoughts holding you back.

You may be wondering what makes your life special or meaningful. It probably will have little to do with material goods or how much money you have acquired. It will instead be about your spirit, your soul, your morals, your sense of integrity, that place inside you that defines your core, how you view yourself, your origins and your worldview.

This is a question you can delve into because it is a question that has an answer that will always be your answer. That answer makes it *your* truth, as it pertains to your life and is answered by you. No one else has to approve it and it doesn't require any further anxiety.

Feeling the spirit within your soul, being who you are with compassion and acceptance, will allow you to feel and experience delight. The spiritual side of life is yours for the taking, and it belongs to you. It is your perception, your way of looking at your life on a different level of consciousness—one beyond yourself, the daily grind, and the automatic responses to your routines.

Carolyn, a writing coach and friend, came in from Texas with her daughter to partake in the wild beauty of the state. She spent a night at the Ghost Ranch, a retreat center frequented by Georgia O'Keeffe and other artists wanting a special place to paint the gorgeous colors of the landscape that surrounds this area. She told me they stayed in a cottage above the library.

"We were right above the twenty-four-hour library! That meant I could go downstairs and sit in the midst of ancient books with ancient words about this land, about life, and death. And I could do this at 2:00 a.m. if I wanted to. It was like winning a lottery. I told my seventeen-year-old daughter about it and she just rolled over and went back to sleep."

She seemed as excited as many people would be if they were staying above a twenty-four-hour bar that served liquor all night. But this friend is special and spiritual beyond any definition. A library in a sacred locale was for her a most spiritual and revered place.

We continued our conversation as we sat outdoors on a restaurant patio here in Santa Fe. Carolyn began looking around at the wide expanse of skies.

"The sky is beautiful here. Do you ever get tired of it?" Carolyn asked. I thought it an odd question and yet I know how it can be to take one's own land for granted if you have been there a long time.

"Never. I never get tired of these colorful skies with cloud formations that fill the spirit. It is such a spiritual and joyful experience just to drive to work." While she considered my statement, she added what she felt the draw to New Mexico was all about.

"You know, when I had access to those books at that library I noticed that many were very old books, some books of poems, some written by Native Americans. But all of them had the same theme, life *and* death. They wrote about the connection to the ancient ruins, the pueblos, graveyards, and the spirit of living and of dying. The words beautifully portrayed that bond to the land, the earth, ashes to ashes, dust to dust. There was so much soul in those words."

We looked at each other with the same wide-eyed grin. It was that primeval connection that draws so many people to New Mexico. That connection you can feel in your heart and sense in your soul despite being so hard to explain out loud. It exists outside of you and from within simultaneously.

The lay of the land and the beauty of the skies is an awe that is magical beyond words, and that sense of connection can be felt anywhere in nature, in any place at any time.

Can you allow yourself to see your life with a third eye? See the natural beauty of the landscape right outside your home? The trees rustling in the breeze, a sunrise, a sunset, butterflies that have been freed from their cocoons, the wonder and glory of the universe? What do you feel and experience at that moment?

"We have to dare to be ourselves, however frightening or strange that self may prove to be." — *May Sarton*

At this stage of life, self-consciousness is the antithesis of the spirit, our spirit. We no longer need to worry what someone else thinks of us, a first stage worry, or whether our opinion is different than a friend's about politics or even religion. It *will* be different. If you have really explored what your beliefs are in your journaling and writing, your beliefs will not be exactly the same as another's way of thinking. They will be your self-examined thoughts and views. It is time to be the you that you always wanted to be, without worry of judgment, your own or someone else's.

My husband used to frequent a hardware store in North Texas when he was in his teens. He remembers seeing a seventyish-year-old man named Mr. Sanchez sitting at the back of the store, feet propped up on a desk, smoking Cuban cigars; it was not very unusual in that day and time, the 60's, to be smoking in your own store.

What was unusual was that Mr. Sanchez had pink surgical tape holding his skin back from his eyebrows to his forehead, from the corner of his eyes to the side of his face, and from both jowls to his ears. This was a common occurrence, not a one-time event. Hearing this story, my first reaction was that he must have had an injury that caused scars which he needed to cover with tape.

Though it might have been just what it appeared to be, an older man, with loose skin, who wanted to do something non-invasive and non-surgical about it. This would be the epitome of a lack of self-consciousness, or maybe more of a lack of awareness. While a number of us have looked in the mirror and held an index finger and thumb on our face, pulling upward to raise the loose skin to remind ourselves of how we used to look, Mr. Sanchez's way would be an extreme measure to look younger.

What courage and aplomb it would take to not care what others thought and just be. Maybe his tape was invisible to him and when he looked in the mirror, it faded away and all he saw was the youthful visage of his past.

My college suitemate never seemed self-conscious. At nineteen and in the first half of life, she seemed soulful beyond her years. We met our freshman year in our coed dorm at Colorado State. Her soul was really confidence, a confidence that comes from being the only girl in a stable household with two older brothers. She exuded brashness and a coolness that eluded me. We took French and Sociology classes together and she excelled in both.

One time in our Sociology of Society and Change class, she breezed in past the instructor saying how she was late but didn't care and needed to talk to him about a previous class that he held. Could she bring this up now, she asked, in front of the entire class?

I sat in the back, my normal and customary seat, especially when you have social anxiety and would really rather not be noticed by anyone, much less the professor.

I had no idea that she was up to anything. We hadn't communicated earlier about her staging an experiment, so that well-known fear of the unknown crept up on me as she loudly voiced her complaints.

Really, I don't have much memory of *what* she said, just how she said it. It was loud and aggressive to this passive and anxiety-ridden student. Despite being her friend, I knew she could fell me at any time with her acerbic wit and intelligence. You could say without a doubt that she was not shy.

This, what I would call a tirade, lasted about three minutes in which she berated the professor for doing whatever it was she thought he did, and he took it without defending himself.

Until he asked for other student reactions, and we heard almost all of the other students side with the professor. But I do remember one or two taking Kris's side. That was the experiment. To see if anyone else would stand up to an authority figure and chime in with an aggressive vocal student in front of the class.

Of course, I knew what my reaction would be. "How can she do that? I would never, *could* never do that." Well my point in this episodic memory is to say that now, at this stage of life, it is time to have soul, live our life, stand up to anyone who abuses or bullies us, and defend our beliefs.

But the other side of that coin is to say that you may not need to. You have a choice. If you know what and how you believe, there is also the option to keep it to yourself because it needs no defense, just quiet acceptance of your own understanding.

IF I KEEP DRIVING IN CIRCLES, I KNOW A CLOSER PARKING SPACE WILL APPEAR.

You know those occurrences that happen when we least expect them, like driving into a crowded and what appears to be full parking lot and finding a space right in front of a grocery store? You may have so much on your mind and be in a place of somewhere else that you may not notice the small events that occur as gifts to make our day easier. You may notice them but think you just got lucky.

You can exercise your spirit by becoming aware of those small events that happen each day and see them as gifts from the universe. I once asked a fifty-five-year-old client, Darlene, to make a list of all the small blessings that had befallen her the week before she came in for our appointment. Darlene tended to live everywhere but in the present and often stayed anxious with worried thoughts of her future. I wanted her to think about what positive events she may have missed while she worried so much about her future.

She proudly brought in her homework the following session, a page filled with fifteen incidents that had happened to her. Some of the events she listed included finding a scarf she thought she had lost in her dresser drawer, being late for work but finding a place to park right in front of her office, how being late had her miss a call from a client but her boss took the call instead and the client had a chance to tell the boss how much he liked working with his employee, how her grouchiness turned around when she passed a homeless women on the street who smiled at her.

Darlene said none of these had happened that week before I had asked her to focus. Instead, she said these events happened the week of our next appointment. It was because she had an assignment to do and was encouraged to be in the present with this task. She actually taught herself to be in the present this way, as she had fun looking for these in-the-moment joys.

By being in the moment, you can find positive events that can bring enjoyment to your day. It is the small, in-the-present events in which we experience happiness. The large celebratory occasions like weddings, births, job offerings, graduations, home buying, European vacations, or bucket list items only occur sporadically throughout our lives. The smaller daily moments that bring us smiles are the ones that sustain us and can bring us lasting joy.

Vera, Chuck and Dave

Music is another way we can exercise our spirit and reduce anxiety. Music can transform us and change our mood from negative to positive with just a lyric, a melody, or both. Can you identify from which Beatles song those three names came? I couldn't. Not until I read the entire lyrics. While I have sung the song many times to myself or hummed along when I didn't quite know or understand the words, I never knew these names were part of that song, "When I'm Sixty-Four."

Often, we hear a song and it transports us back to another decade and we are filled with memories from that time. We might cry, smile, or laugh just by humming a Frankie Valli tune, "You're just too good to be true. Can't take my eyes off of you...."

What a blessing to be able to experience this phenomenon. Truly, this is a gift from *somewhere* and however we describe this wondrous happening, it feeds our soul. No matter how you define or experience the spirit, we are moved by music; it is part of the natural human beauty that lies within each of us.

My sister and I used music to calm our fears and keep us from worrying about our future. We didn't understand that as kids, we just knew how free we felt whenever we would listen to Red Foxx on our parents' record player. His words made us laugh and his music had us giggling on the floor in our downstairs living room, the same living room that had the piano on which we played duets like "Heart and Soul," over and over again. The repetition soothed our soul, calmed our fears and could keep any anxiety at bay, at least for a moment in time.

"Time may change me, but I can't trace time." — *David Bowie, Changes*

The fear of change and what this time of life has to offer can be scary and take us out of the moment. When we are afraid, we don't see those small blessings and don't experience the spirit-filled wonder of our souls. Change is a moving on from the routines we knew, even if those routines were chaotic or negative. It is now different. What makes us put a negative connotation on *different*?

If we can challenge the notion that we should be fearful of change, we can embrace it. Even though every change is a loss, a loss of what was and what we were used to, that loss is also a new beginning with new possibilities. If you see change as a prospect of something new or different, as in a new beginning, you can accept uncertainty and not fear the unknown.

In fact, one way to rise above ourselves is when we do something new and different by seeking out novel experiences. Abraham Maslow, an American psychologist, describes in his book *Motivation and Personality* a hierarchy of needs that man must attain in order, whereby basic human needs such as food, water, and sleep must be met before the higher need for safety, love and belonging, self-esteem, and self-actualization, can be available to us. He describes self-actualization as a desire for self-fulfillment and to be all that we can be. It is a person's need to be and do that for which the person has a vocation. It is a "calling," a full expression of his or her creative potential.

Within that top tier of needs, he mentions the need for peak experiences, which he defines as a "tremendous intensification of any of the experiences in which there is loss of self or transcendence of [self]." He calls it an ecstatic emotional experience likened to what a person might call a euphoric "mystical experience" where there is a blending of heart and mind.

A peak experience can be something as big as a sense of life beyond ours as you scale a mountain top, sail the ocean, parasail or skydive. A spiritual awakening could happen when flying in a plane, meeting an elder family member from your country of origin for the first time, or being with someone as they make the transition from life to death.

Whether you call a state of joy a peak experience, a mystical experience, a moment of transformation, a spiritual awakening, or an instant of grace, it is a soul-filled place in which you are being you and feeling that connection outside yourself. These moments are fleeting and not sustained, yet the joy and peace of mind that can come from them can be.

If you can learn to embrace new experiences or any changes that may come as a result of those new experiences, then you can allow yourself to see the benefits from them. When you can appreciate change and its various possibilities, then you can alleviate the anxiety, worry and "what ifs" and look forward to whatever the newness brings.

You can then ask yourself the question, "I wonder how my life will be different?" and be excited about what the future may hold. For example, if your child marries within another culture and they move far from home, instead of worrying about how often you may see them, consider how it exciting it might be to learn about their customs and to visit them in the spouse's country of origin.

You can say yes to life, without blurting it out. But, if you need to blurt it out because yes has been a foreign word to you, then say "YES!" Be in the moment by feeling whatever it is you feel, dance in the streets, sing along with a song on the radio in your car, and let your spirit come alive. It will break through any anxiety that impedes you and allow you to appreciate the instant and the freedom you have to choose how to respond to that moment.

The result is self-acceptance and can liberate you from unwanted worry about how you appear to others. Freeing your mind of all the worries, angst, and what other people might be thinking of you can allow you to be you, the unique, one-of-a-kind, spirited YOU.

And at our age, no one is really watching anyway. If they are, so what?

Just be yourself. Enjoy the present moment.

ACTION PLAN

1. Why are you here? What brings you meaning? What is your purpose, a purpose that only you can fill and only you can define? How is it manifesting itself in your life? Is there anxiety in knowing your purpose? In not knowing your purpose? What is true to you?

2. If you aren't sure what that purpose is, go to a place of stillness, a quiet place, a silent retreat by yourself or with others, and meditate on it. Stillness activates the body and self-healing repair mechanisms. Ask yourself the question. Listen to the response. Write down what you don't like to do or what appalls you or makes you cringe. So, does that mean you like the opposite of that, or something in between? If you don't know what you like or just

what you were meant to do, explore what you
know you were not meant to do.

3. What is keeping you from that place of spirit
    where you can feel your inner joy and soulful
    intent?

4. What do you believe happens to you after you
    die? Do you believe in Heaven? Hell? God?
    Do you believe you have the answers to life?
    Or do you feel like you have more questions
    than answers? Can you be at peace with that?

5. What does spirituality mean to you? What
    does it mean to you to live with soul? If you
    feel that you live with soul, how does it mani-
    fest itself in your daily life?

8

HOMEGROWN ANXIETY

"Factual knowledge is power, self knowledge is empowering."
Sue Legacy

Home is that place we grew up, the place where all the good, the bad and the ugly of our youth happened, that place which housed those people who shaped and molded us into the human beings we are today. Our parents, grandparents, siblings, friends, aunts, uncles, cousins, teachers, and clergy all contributed to the seeds of the anxious selves in our childhood that create the anxious selves we are now. Home was a source of our greatest joys, some of our deepest pain, and the points of origin for most of our anxieties.

If your anxiety has not ceased and it is as strong as in the first stage of your life, if you feel that you are bad or feel shame about being who you are, if you are unable to forgive a wrong done to you or a wrong which you have done to someone else, if you see your past life as all bad, then you must go back home. Again. Now.

By going home, I mean that you have to delve into your past hurts, anger and disgrace that continue to cause you anxiety so that you can be freed from the strongholds of shame.

In his novel *You Can't Go Home Again*, Thomas Wolfe tells the story of George Webber, the protagonist who writes about his childhood home life. When he returns to his town after his book is published, he is treated with disdain and outrage for exposing the town's naked truths.

His truth about how you can't go home again reveals how difficult it is to go back to a place that has changed just as we have changed, along with all the remaining family members and participants. For Webber, when he is scorned, he leaves feeling shamed and moves on to discover the world outside his smaller existence. After he spends some time away in Europe during World War II, he comes back and creates a new narrative; his life is different and he is filled with a broader range of emotions, perspective about his life, and a fresh worldview.

Many people try to forget about the past. "It's over, it happened and who wants to relive it. Not me." To delve into your past to determine what might be keeping you in a place of despair, especially now in your later years, may seem scary and frightening. It might be that you don't remember a lot about your past but what you do remember haunts you.

Or you may remember a lot, not much of it positive. You may have scenes in your head of Dad abusing Mom, or of a sibling's emotional abuse and fury towards you or another sibling. You may cringe when you think about a drunken rage from a parent of which you were the target and how you felt diminished and powerless. You may have heard a lot of cursing and yelling and just want to get that out of your head.

The key is whether you are still hurting and anxious about a past wound. If, in this stage of life you continue to be preoccupied with something that happened in the home of your past, that you believe you should not *still* be worried about, now is the time to find a way to heal.

OBSTACLES TO HEAL FROM ANXIETY

One of the barriers that keep people our age from seeking help with lingering anxiety or worries about past issues is that working on anxiety takes too much time. You may never have liked the idea of going to a therapist during your earlier life and now you don't see how it could be useful. Besides, you have so much to do with your grown kids, grandkids, friends, that part-time job, classes you want to take at the community college, even a course you want to teach in continuing education.

You may not want to take the time to use a tool that will help you with any rumination you have. You only think about past issues right before bed, or if you have had a fight with your spouse, or if you had one too many cocktails and are embarrassed about your behavior the next day.

Or maybe you have been to a therapist or several in your life span. Maybe they were not helpful and you are still in a place of worry and fret about the past, or the future.

Maybe you have a parent's thought in your head, "Get over it! Stop blaming someone else for all that old stuff and get on with your life."

But sometimes we just can't get over that stuff. We may first need to venture back to the origins of the pain and hurt that continues to make us anxious. There are ways to get to the heart of what continues to trouble you without going to a therapist for years. Of course, going to therapy can be very helpful, though think of it as an option, not a necessity, for healing. Whether you go to therapy as an adjunct to these methods or not, the outcome is self-awareness, forgiveness, compassion and healing, from anxiety, worry and fear.

Another barrier that comes between anxiety and getting help for it is that there is too much information out there. How will I know which method is best? What is going to work for me? What approach do I utilize? You might say, "I don't have time to do the research or look on the Internet. Have you seen all those options and alternatives for getting rid of my worry and anxiety? My goodness, it is just too overwhelming.

"And besides," you might say, "the main barrier is my own thoughts. All I have to do is change my negative thoughts to more positive ones and I'll be okay. I know I say some pretty mean stuff to myself. I can get over it. Look, I have made it this far, haven't I?"

Yes, you have. And that is huge. But you can leave those worries back in the past if you face them, address them and understand what they are trying to tell you. Then you will be able to experience this part of your life with less angst, more calm and compassion for yourself and what you went through.

There is a theory called Validation Theory developed by Naomi Feil, a social worker who grew up in a nursing home, then called Homes for the Aged, where her father was the administrator and her mother the head of the Social Services department. After working with the elderly, she developed her own tenets about what she called "old-old" people with diminished mental capacities.

One principle she held was that behavior in the very old is not just about the changes in the brain but also the physical, psychological, and social changes that take place over one's lifespan. She is saying that if you or a loved one get some form of dementia, it may be due to brain changes, but within those brain changes lie the fermented combination of past experiences that you have had throughout your life.

She also subscribes to the belief that if someone express-es painful feelings that are acknowledged and validated by a trusted listener, those feelings will diminish. Furthermore, if painful feelings are ignored or suppressed, they will gain strength.

Essentially what she theorizes is that if you deal with your past issues before you become mentally incapacitated, you will not express the anger, sadness and emotional pain that comes with *not* dealing with past issues.

We do not know whether if you manage any lingering past issues and you get dementia or Alzheimer's that you will not be angry and resentful or combative to others. However, we do know that you can live a happier, more joyful life *right now* if you do.

A friend's mother was diagnosed with Alzheimer's demen-tia over ten years ago. As her illness progressed, she was placed into an assisted care facility, and then a nursing home, and now is on a locked unit solely for dementia patients. She often forgets dates, her own birthday, when she ate last, and whether her parents and siblings are alive. Her physical health is poor and she often falls due to balance issues and needs emergency care. She was put on hospice when the doc-tor determined her life prognosis was six months or less.

After that six-month period, when it appeared that she would continue to be alive for an undetermined amount of time, she was taken off hospice. She has always had a good sense of humor and was never combative. Her family listens to her repetitive stories with as much humor as they can.

In contrast, a client's eighty-eight-year-old mother-in-law has had Alzheimer's for about the same amount of time, is physically healthy and currently lives in a nursing home specific to this disease. She has been angry, combative, cursing, and needed medication to subdue her. When it seemed that she was *too* sedated, she was taken off her medications. This resulted in worse behavior than prior to her medication. She was put back on different ones, which she takes to this day.

I have knowledge of both of these women's backgrounds; both had some past trials and tribulations for which today's woman would seek help: alcoholism of a spouse, rage and anger from a spouse, and affairs within marriage. Yet, one woman seems to flourish and outlast many of her peers with a sense of humor and compassion.

The other woman is in a state of medication for her socially unacceptable behaviors. This comparison of similar situations with very different behaviors can be theorized in a number of ways. Yet, the point I want to make here is that we don't know what state we will be in or whether a particular theory will hold water for us and help us when we get to that place we go before we go.

But we can work on the Now. The Now is all we have before we leave this earth. Open your heart for more peace on earth before you go back to your forever home.

There is a poem by Linda Ellis called "The Dash." If you have never heard it recited, here is a link to it: www.linda-ellis.com/the-dash-the-dash-poem-by-linda-ellis-.html.

It describes the amount of time between our birth and our death as a *dash*. Her poignant message encourages us to spend that time wisely, without anger, fear, or worry, and more appreciation and joy.

My sister asked that this poem be read at our mother's funeral. At the time, I was still holding on to some hurt between my sister and me and told her that we needed to focus on our mother and her life at our services, not the universal life that we all share.

It took many years before I saw the value of that poem read at our mother's memorial. It has meaning for us all. When one of us dies, a piece of the whole dies with us. We all will go home, whatever home means to us, at some point.

GO HOME THROUGH JOURNALING TO FIND PEACE OF MIND

"Letting go gives us freedom, and freedom is the only condition for happiness. If, in our heart, we still cling to anything— anger, anxiety, or possession—we cannot be free."— ThichN-hatHanh, The Heart of the Buddha's Teaching: Transforming Suffering into Peace, Joy and Liberation

"How do I know what I think until I see what I say?"—E.M. Forster, English novelist and short-story writer

One of the ways that we can go home at this stage of our lives is through our writing. Writing takes us back to an event, incident, or past happening *slowly*. When we start writing, we are not sure just how it will turn out or even what we will write about. We may start to journal about one topic and find ourselves on another.

We may think we feel one way about a past event, only to find that we feel differently than what we initially thought. We can have insights into our own and others' behaviors. These insights can alter decades of faulty thinking. We may still find a traumatic event distasteful, yet discover some underlying factors that can change our perspective. That new perspective can lessen the hurt, soothe the pain, and ultimately decrease the anxiety that we carried with us for so long.

My very first foray into journaling was in the early 70's. I was a sophomore in college, had moved from my dorm into the off-campus College Inn ready to meet and make new friends. In my freshman year, I had a room at the end of the hall and didn't really get to know any other girls on my floor except for my suitemates. I didn't pledge a sorority and my roommate was more obsessed with her back-home boyfriend than with making new friends. I thought going to this type of dormitory would provide me with more opportunity to make friends. I was wrong.

At this coed living facility, we all had private rooms and no one seemed to hang out in the common areas. I became homesick, isolated and lonely. Somehow, I began to write, a lot, daily and whenever the mood struck. It struck often. I wrote about my sadness, loneliness, anxiety, and fear of what was in front of me: the unknown! I was only eighteen and in my second year of college.

I bought a spiral notebook and wrote down my feelings whenever they felt like they would burst from my core. I filled several journals. The writing process provided me with a sense of comfort and safety. I had an outlet and a friend—myself—to whom I could tell anything—my deepest and darkest thoughts.

After a while, I noticed a light shining on some of my words. My mood improved, my worries decreased. I got out of my dark funk. I remember feeling empowerment, a new feeling that replaced the powerlessness that I had felt for so long.

Journaling and writing about your life is transforming and healing. But what you write about and how you write are important. You can write abstractly and just sit down and write whatever comes out. Or you can think of a relationship that has been especially difficult for you, events like a graduation, the first day of school, a day you were bullied by an older classmate, or a wedding where someone gave a toast or said something that was offensive or hurtful. Or you can journal about an emotion that just doesn't seem to go away, like anger, hurt or sadness, which hides underneath all the anxiety that has risen to the top of how you deal with those underlying emotions.

Writing about some of the painful memories that stuck with me for years helped me let go of them and see them in a different light. One of these times was in May of 1969 when my divorced parents attended my high school graduation together.

To have them both there was especially nerve-racking because my father could squelch any positive feelings I might have for myself, and that day I was feeling pretty good about my life. I was on high alert for a possible verbal altercation that might affect my proud feelings.

The ceremony was held outside on a warm breezy day. I had let my hair grow several inches down my back—almost to my waist and it had been ironed straight just hours before. Ironing your hair was the 60's version of the flat iron.

As my name was called, I stood up from my seat and walked over to our headmaster, who presented me with a gold and black piece of paper. I still trembled in front of a group and this day was no exception. Since I didn't have to say anything to the crowd, I uttered a "Thank you" to our presenter and headed down the aisle to my new life. I was afraid to look over at my parents so I kept my head down as I passed the row where they were seated. I worried that instead of a proud smile there might be another look from them that would tarnish my poise.

I heard a loud comment from my father. I kept my head to the ground instead of up in the warm air where it belonged.

"Why doesn't she cut that hair?" he said just to my mother, or maybe he intended all the parents and the entire crowd to hear him. Maybe if everyone heard his dismay about my appearance, he wouldn't be so embarrassed by whatever he saw in me that did not please him. I felt my face scrunch into what had become an automatic expression by then—disillusionment that I had disappointed him no matter how hard I tried otherwise. It was my attempt to keep the sting of my father's remark from piercing through me on this supposed-to-be-pristine day.

I moved quickly down the aisle and waited at the back for a familiar face to greet. I wanted to avoid any more negative thoughts about myself and decided to stuff them further down inside my soul. Instead of allowing myself to cry, I made small talk about how excited I was to graduate and have a new beginning.

One of the helpful outcomes of that writing was to see how I came to enter college with that continued shame that I was not doing something right and how my fears and anxieties entered college right along with me. Through writing I could process moments that I had carried with me for years, and find an understanding of my anxiety, fears of presenting myself to the world, and from where they came. With each story written, I gained insights into those painful memories and could build a new narrative to let go of any power they held over me.

When we journal we can record these occurrences, experiences, observations, reflections, memories, insights, opinions, and feelings on paper. Many people have likened it to a diary, like the one you may have kept, locked and hidden in your closet.

Mine was pink with a smiling teen in a ponytail on the front faux-leather cover. It remains locked, key left in the lock, stuffed inside a box of memorabilia in a guest bedroom closet. It is like a window to my preteen years; superficial and immature in thought, without mention of any household turmoil, just boy-crazed reflections and of concern to no one but this young girl's inner mind.

THE JOYS OF JOURNALING

"In moments of ecstasy, in moments of despair the journal remains an impassive, silent friend, forever ready to coach, to comfort, to intrigue, to critique, to console. Its potential as a tool for holistic mental health is unsurpassed." - Kathleen Adams, therapeutic writer, author and psychotherapist

Studies show how writing can help improve asthma, Rheumatoid arthritis, and has more recently shown how regular writing or journaling can strengthen immune cells or T-lymphocytes. James Pennebaker, Professor of Psychology at University of Texas-Austin, author of two books and over fifty research studies correlating expressive writing and physiological and emotional healing, has this to say about journaling: "Writing about emotional upheavals in our lives can improve physical and mental health."

Writing about an experience or relationship can give you a new perspective and meaning about its presence in your life. It can bring your unconscious thoughts and feelings to the surface. Journaling as therapy can be used to express difficult material. Or you can access previously inaccessible material. Both Freud and Jung used journal writing as an adjunct to their psychoanalytic approach.

Ira Progoff, a New York City psychologist who studied with Carl Jung, began using journal writing as a complement to his psychotherapy. He developed methods that have been used in the prison system for inmates. Inmate testimonials have mentioned how journaling helped them heal from the pain they carried throughout their lives, and allowed them to be able to confront and conquer the demons from the past.

"The unconscious mind is decidedly simple, unaffected, straightforward and honest. It hasn't got all of this facade, this veneer of what we call adult culture. It's rather simple, rather childish... It is direct and free."— Milton H. Erickson, M.D.

This is a large part of what writing is all about. It gets to your subconscious. You can let go of any pretenses of how you think you *should* be and listen as your inner self lets you know who you *really* are. It's a creative, fun way to get to know yourself which can bring you great joy. Journaling is a journey you take with yourself. It is a mindful, in-the-moment experience you can have any time you take pen or pencil to paper.

It can also bring up blocked emotions about experiences that have gone unattended. If you have not been able to grieve a loss, had trauma or shame-based issues without healing, the feelings may be deep inside, not readily accessible or felt. This loss may be causing you physical pain, emotional pain or a flatness of mood and affect that impairs your well-being. When you bring up the source of the pain, it can help alleviate that anxiety that has covered your core for so long.

There are no rules in journaling. No need to worry about penmanship (if you are journaling via computer that is not a concern), grammar, or words you don't know how to spell (again not a worry on a computer). Just write. Writing in a notebook with a pencil or pen can be a way to literally allow the rhythm of the movement to flow onto the page. You can do the same on a computer, only with a readily accessible delete or back button.

I didn't return to journaling until much later—these last ten years. After losing my mom, I decided to write about our relationship as a tribute to her.

Once I began to write of our life together, that one chapter turned into many. I began a natural move from writing about our relationship to writing about other important yet conflicted relationships that shaped me. All of that writing about my life turned my anxieties to a gratitude for my life from which a joy sprang up.

A client in one of my writing classes said that he needs to write for twenty minutes or more to get to a deeper level. For him, any lesser amount of time doesn't go beyond any superficial thinking. You may find that too. Allow yourself at least twenty minutes to delve into the unconscious mind from which your soul will burst forth. You can go from anxiety, pain and hurt to gratitude and joy.

Abstract journaling, or simply writing your thoughts as they come up about a particular topic, is meaningful and a passageway into self-discovery. You can also start with more structured and less abstract writing. This can take you quickly to your unconscious mind, which is where the knowing and the healing from anxiety can begin, and can lead you to more intuitive ways to gain insight into your past and your present beliefs.

Writing is powerful. It is an inner journey that allows you to explore your beliefs on an unconscious level to make you more aware of what you truly think, feel and know. You can explore your truths, find the wisdom and creative nature inside you that you never knew you had, and lessen or alleviate any lingering anxiety from the past. Through your writing, you can go back home and return again with a new awareness of who you are, one with less anxiety and more joy.

ACTION PLAN

1. What comes up when you think about home? What does home mean to you?

2. Can you see how both the positive and the negative aspects of growing up have shaped you?

3. What still brings you anxiety related to your home? What brings you joy?

4. What are some of your positive childhood memories? What were some of the outdoor games you played? Board games? Black-and-white television shows watched?

5. Write down your thoughts and feelings about these questions. Go for twenty minutes. What surprises you about this writing exercise as you read over your discoveries?

9

POWER TO THE ANXIOUS PEOPLE!

*"Everything great in the world comes from neurotics. They alone
have founded our religions and composed our masterpieces."*
Marcel Proust

The seeds of our values are implanted in our family of origin. Our values sprout, germinate and flourish into full-grown standards of behavior. They mature as we develop and become adults.Our values can empower or oppress us. They can encourage our growth or impede us from expansion. If we are aware of the values that we bring with us into adulthood, and we find them important and meaningful for us to maintain, then we can carry them with us from our first stage of life into this later stage of our existence. Without an awareness and clarity of what we value, we may have difficulty with decisions, become confused and anxious, uncertain how to find the peace and joy we seek. If we are unclear about the principles we stand for, it may be difficult to live with integrity and feel whole within ourselves.

Once we identify our values and our principles are aligned with our priorities, we can live in integrity, decrease our anxiety and find our joy and wonder in this time of our lives.

Exploring your values gives you the insight into how you may be responding to your own family now. You may have tried to maintain some values within your family of origin that now cause you anxiety and make you feel off kilter when you cannot maintain them.

For example, you may carry the childhood belief that eating dinner around the dining room table as a family is an important way to stay connected. You want your family to learn gratitude for their food, other family members, their day and how you support them financially through your work.

Yet, when your husband, wife, children or grandchildren do not comply with your requests of daily dinners, which have lately turned into demands, you get angry and upset. You feel anxious and worried that no one cares how much effort you put into dinnertime. You get resentful. You may begin to think about past hurts or what your future will be like without your expectations being met. You may feel unempowered, powerless and hopeless—that future worry that nothing will ever be different and you are destined to a life of despair.

To combat these hopeless anxious feelings, an important task is to discover what you really cherish and whether you are subscribing to those values, or whether your time and actions actually demonstrate something different. Being in sync with your values and how you actually live your life will decrease any anxiety you have more than if you are *not* in sync with your ideals.

It seemed that family-orientedness was an important value in the 50's. At least that is what black-and-white television shows portrayed. Families gathered around the kitchen table at dinnertime, discussed school, household rules, outdoor play, and bedtime. A time for togetherness and breaking bread around the kitchen table was cherished, a chance for a daily recap and to recoup any wholeness that might be lost during your day.

If you watched *Leave it to Beaver,* you might remember Mrs. Cleaver, in her high heels and stylish dress, bring food to the table while Wally, Beaver and Ward eagerly wait to be served their full-course meal. If Eddie Haskell, Wally's passive-aggressive friend, joined them, he would graciously place his napkin in his lap without being reminded as he nudged Wally in how to please and pacify Mr. and Mrs. Cleaver.

I idolized this type of dinnertime occurrence. Not the characterological traits of Eddie Haskell, but the family gathering around the table seemingly with such joy. It was so different than my own.

We had dinner as a family with both my parents until I was in middle school. What I wanted was dinnertime to be a chance to reflect on my day, express myself without reprimand, talk about school, ask questions, and a chance for my siblings and me to feel valued, respected and encouraged.

Instead, before our parents' divorce, dinnertime was a time for lectures to scold us about what we were doing wrong. My father would see this as discipline intended to mold us into well-mannered adults.

"Stop feeding the dog! Eat your meat for God's sake, Cynthia, and stop hiding it under your bread. You're not fooling anybody with that covered-up business. Sit up straight. Don't slouch. Eat your green beans. There are starving children in China who would love to have your green beans."

Of course, under our breaths, we would whisper, "They can have them. How do we get these beans to them?"

If you are finding it hard to feel empowered, are feeling anxious much of the time and are not certain what might be creating those feelings, let's look at some values that might be helpful to allow for a healthier balance.

GRATITUDE, OR WHO WANTS TO SAY THE BLESSING?

"Gratitude turns what we have into enough, and more. It turns denial into acceptance, chaos into order, confusion into clarity...it makes sense of our past, brings peace for today, and creates a vision for tomorrow." – Melody Beattie

"Piglet noticed that even though he had a Very Small Heart, it could hold a rather large amount of Gratitude."— A. A. Milne, Winnie-the-Pooh

Is gratitude one of your values?

As children, it seemed that the only time "thanks" was offered to anyone was during the blessing spoken aloud to God thanking him for our meal. Except for Eddie Haskell's overly polite ways of thanking Mrs. Cleaver for dinner, and his appreciation for birthing her two sons, gratitude for our lives was passé.

We were encouraged, maybe even forced, into the belief that we *should* be grateful for the bounty of vegetables placed on our plate. After all, there were all of those starving children in those underdeveloped countries, not to mention, as no one ever did, all the starving children in our very own United States.

But now, we know differently. We often do feel more gratitude about our lives. At times our fears or worries get in the way and overpower our sense of appreciation. We just forget to express it, feel it, and share it. We may say the blessing, or not. We may not eat at the same time as the rest of our family so we don't even have that moment to remember any blessings, be it food or otherwise.

There is an interesting thing about gratitude and that is that when you appreciate some aspect of your life, or have appreciation for life, you can not be afraid at the same time. Brain studies have shown that a sense of gratitude and fear can not exist in the brain simultaneously.

Instead of being fearful or anxious about some past event or some future worry, you are thinking that life is good. And once you experience that emotional state of gratitude, you can have a sense of well-being and a more joyful outlook on life.

In fact, gratitude is so central to our health that once you experience it for yourself, sleep habits improve, thoughts turn more positive, you can manage life transitions with more ease and you may even feel more in control of your life.

As social worker and researcher Brené Brown, PhD, says, "Joyous people are grateful people."

In those moments of gratefulness, admiration, and awe in your life, you are having an in-the-moment experience, one of sheer contentment for what you have. You are not thinking of what you don't have, or what you wish you had more of; you are filled with the spirit of wonder and respect for that which you do.

The other really exciting aspect of gratitude is that when you practice gratitude by exploring all the ways you are thankful, you will naturally zap that fear and anxiety which will open up your ability to *find* the joy you so deserve. You deserve it because you have been introspective and realize you could be less than grateful if you so choose. But rather than choose self-indulgence and want of further gain you can choose to have a perspective of *enough*.

But you may wonder how to be grateful for a life with so many trials and tribulations, or past traumas? If I am having a health crisis, or my family member is having one, how can I be grateful?

You can find what you are grateful for by being still, being in a moment of meditation alone with yourself and listening to your thoughts. If you are in the middle of a crisis and feel sadness and fear about what *might* happen, if you turn inward and allow yourself to let go of all the worried thoughts you may be having, you can get to that place of calm and peace.

If we can acknowledge and be aware of those small blessings we receive each and every day, we can learn how to be grateful for our lives. And often we are grateful for what we have when we see what others do not have. When we compare our situation to others, our situation may not seem nearly as awful.

Being grateful is not either/or. You can be ill with a disease or cancer and be grateful that you caught it in time. If you didn't catch it in a timely fashion, you might be grateful for the rest of your body that works, the fact that you are not bed-bound, that your spouse can help take care of you, that your grandchildren are all healthy. There are as many things to be grateful for as there are of which to fear. Turn those fears and worries into gratitude for what has not happened that you have feared would.

"It is not joy that makes us grateful. It is gratitude that makes us joyful."— Catholic theologian David Steindl-Rast

I never thought that I would be so grateful for our little pet, Nada, after we lost Dixie. Dixie's presence was so comforting and her gentle spirit soothed our household. It was hard to imagine how a much smaller pet could provide the same comfort. Yet, it was that in-the-moment experience with this rambunctious puppy that became one of the most joyous experiences of my life.

Nada had come to greet me upon my return home from work, knocking my footing out from under me. Not wanting to fall on top of her, I managed to wind up right next to her. Now she had free rein to lick my face, ears, mouth and nose. Her greeting was one of joy and unconditional love, so different from the hand slaps that I received in my childhood. I laughed until I cried.

That in-the-moment pleasure brought me an everlasting joy. It was one of those genuine peak experiences. The gratitude for having made this decision to have a small dog in our lives turned this moment into sheer bliss. Any anxiety I had about her turned to joy for this new dear pet and that spontaneous moment of fun.

If you have never experienced the empowerment that gratitude for your life can bring, maybe it is time to incorporate it into your value system.

INTEGRITY

Having integrity in your life is a value that can empower you, help you decrease your anxiety and fears and make you feel whole. There are two definitions of integrity that can be helpful to note. One definition of integrity is "the quality of being honest, honorable, of virtue and decency, having strong moral principles."

The other is "the state of being whole and undivided."

It is said that the way this second definition could be understood is in relation to nations, as in national solidarity and territorial integrity. But the *state* of being whole and undivided can be applied to an individual too. It would mean being aligned with our values, living those values, and doing so without fear of retribution. Instead of being empty and incomplete, you can feel whole and complete. What a sense of joy you could find if you lived in a congruent and integrated way.

Erik Erikson's last stage of development, Ego Integrity vs. Despair, is about the importance of developing this integrity with your values. The empowerment you can gain by feeling that wholeness.

My husband came home from work one cold December day and told me about a man he saw walking barefoot along the main drag in our town. As he headed for lunch and turned into the parking lot of a taco stand he said he had to swerve to miss a rail-thin male standing at the edge of the drive, stock-still except for one hand flicking the air as if bothered by a pesky mosquito. Once inside the restaurant, my husband stared back outside at the man who hadn't moved from his spot by the telephone pole. He couldn't let him stand there in the cold.

"Come on, man, let's get you something to eat," he told him, "and some shoes for God's sake." The man was dressed in a thin windbreaker, ball cap and tattered old work pants, no shoes. His bearded face was streaked with tears either from the cold or his soul, or both. The man said his name was Bobby.

When my husband took him inside to order their food, he said a woman whispered to him, "You're a good man," while she skirted hurriedly around Bobby. Another woman told him, "God bless you, sir," as an elderly man shook his hand, planting a five-dollar bill in his palm. "For shoes," he whispered. "I wish I had more to give you," and he patted Bobby's back as he passed through the door.

They took the food out to my husband's truck to eat while my husband grabbed his spare pair of work boots from the back and told Bobby to put them on. Bobby firmly remarked, "Need socks."

When my husband heard the only request this man had, he knew he had to help him out by getting him something warmer to wear. On the way to the Big Five store, Bobby haltingly said he'd been homeless since 1980 when he was in the hospital getting treatment for his schizophrenia. When the funding ran out for the program, he said he was sent to the Salvation Army, and now for the past thirty-four years he's lived day to day.

They bought some shoes, clothes and a bedroll and then took Bobby to the men's shelter. My husband told him he needed to get out. Tears began streaming down Bobby's face, and then he started sucking in his breath and his cheeks as he stammered and cried more tears. Bobby didn't move from his seat in the truck.

"Bobby, I need to go to a meeting. I can either leave you here or take you to the hospital." Bobby didn't move for several more minutes when my husband said he heard the woman's words from the taco stand in his head, "You're a good man." Then he said he started to cry along with Bobby. Bobby's tears flowed for another five minutes before he got out of the car without uttering a word.

My husband said he never felt like a good man because he just left Bobby at the shelter without helping him more. After a lot of reflection about this, he realized he didn't feel like a good man, despite the very noble act of kindness he offered to Bobby, because he felt impotent to change the way issues like mental health, civil rights, voter rights, women's rights, gun violence, living wages, and the environment have become political pawns instead of democratic and universal rights for all. He may have felt that sense of virtue and decency, yet there was no feeling of being whole and undivided, just incomplete and empty.

There was a sense that he was not living with the full potential of his integrity. He didn't feel like he lived the rest of his life in accordance with his values. He felt a strong pull to do more, to change Bobby's living situation for the better, yet at the same time was unsure how to do so.

I was in awe that my husband took time out of his day to help a fellow human being with the basic elements that we should all expect from our lives. I was in awe of his act of kindness, an act that exuded integrity, an honorable, decent, and humane way to help another person in need without fear of retribution or sanction. While he couldn't change the world with his actions, he could affect change in his own and another man's soul. A change in one man's soul is a change in the universal soul. What a huge difference he may have made in a life.

TRUTH AND HONESTY

"Your time is limited, so don't waste it living someone else's life. Don't be trapped by dogma—which is living with the results of other people's thinking. Don't let the noise of other's opinions drown out your own inner voice. And most important, have the courage to follow your heart and intuition. They somehow already know what you truly want to become. Everything else is secondary." – Steve Jobs

"Believe nothing; no matter where you read it, or who said it, no matter if I have said it, unless it agrees with your own reason and your own common sense."— Buddha

We search for truth in various religions, schools of thought, gurus, the Bible, the Torah, the Quran, our neighbors, our parents, and sometimes even our children. Who's got the truth? How do we find the truth, the real truth and nothing but the truth? What do you believe, and whom?

This conundrum can be especially haunting at this time of our lives because of the shortness of our life span. How can we find comfort and peace, even joy, with all this mental confusion and how will we know when we find it?

Empowerment comes from knowing yourself, finding what you trust and believe, and by living in the integrity of the moment. Only you know if you are being honest with yourself about your real feelings and your thoughts about you and the world around you. Communicating effectively with another person in an assertive way is important, but more important than that is to communicate with yourself in an honest and authentic way.

"The teacher who is indeed wise does not bid you to enter the house of his wisdom but rather leads you to the threshold of your mind." – Khalil Gibran, The Prophet

What motivates you? Think about what you do each day. Is it what you want to be doing? If it isn't, what makes you continue to do it? Monetary concerns, pressure from a spouse, pressure from an adult child, the "shoulds," the commitment to yourself to persevere despite the consequences (which would mean that perseverance is a value of yours), to never quit what you start, old adages of your parents, fear of the unknown?

Knowing yourself will allow you to be in a place of harmony with your beliefs, your feelings, your world and the present moment, the only place there is peace.

Peace means no anxiety

When you really know and understand your motivations and intentions, you will like being with yourself, for you will be living with integrity, as a whole and complete human being. You will respect that person in the mirror. You will be able to connect with yourself and be alone without feeling lonely. You will not always have to be with others to obtain that reflection of how you want to be seen. That wondrous *both and*, not *either/or*. You can find your voice by listening to you and to the universe, in whatever way that occurs to you. That is your truth.

Knowing what is true to you and being honest with yourself leads to your very own wisdom. Wisdom is the quality of having the experience, the knowledge and the good judgment as you make a decision.

There is a psychotherapeutic approach called Dialectic Behavior Therapy, or DBT. One aspect of this approach is its tenet about the Wise Mind. Marsha Linehan, the creator of DBT, says that our wise mind is the intersection of our emotional state with our rational state.

To be wise is to utilize your experiences from your life, the knowledge you have acquired, and your judgment to determine healthy decisions. Our gut is a crucial aspect of wisdom. It is like a blending of heart, mind, and soul. When you are centered in that blended place it is there you will find your wisdom.

Age doesn't take everything away; it gives something back too. Throughout the years of life's experiences, pain, instability, falling, getting up, we earn wisdom. Even though we may not have the answers to those major questions of why or how we are here, it is now okay. Even without answers, we can be more open to what is, and more available to experience our life in the present moment.

Look beyond the wrinkles, dimpling skin, and thinning hair.

Look inside. See the person you really are—that glorious inner beauty, gratitude for life, and wise mind.

Human Connection

When you look at the ways young people in their first stage of life connect these days through texting, Instagram, Facebook, Skype, and YouTube, you might think it impersonal and distant. We grew up with landlines, long-distance fees and a spanking for calling beyond our local boundaries. We are just becoming used to email, the newer version of letter-writing or card-sending, while these shorter, less personal methods are becoming more mainstream and acceptable. Texting is so mainstream that it may be the only way some parents connect with their children, or grandchildren. It is so commonplace that there are new rules in the dating arena related to texting to make a date, break a date, or end a relationship.

Texting is so abundant in our culture that now we have laws prohibiting the act while driving. In my hometown a law was just passed that poses fines to text or even to check emails while in stopped traffic.

All these newfangled ways to communicate seem to lessen the connection we seek. When something goes askew with the technological aspect of any of these handheld computer modes of communicating, our anxiety can go sky-high right along with the inability to reach the ones with whom we were trying to connect.

For us baby boomers, a beeper was the way that Big Brother could find us wherever, doing whatever it was we were doing. My first job after graduate school as a social worker and discharge planner was at the eight-story Atlanta Baptist Medical Center. Our offices were half a mile from the main hospital, and our assigned floors could be both the eighth floor and the first floor ICU, or even the basement Coronary Care Unit.

Our beepers, along with that anxiety, were a constant companion and rarely ended up inside the large pockets of our white lab coats. We kept them in one hand while we dialed the phone with the other. When our beeper went off, we either ran directly to the floor from which the call came, or hurried to the nearest landline to call for our next directive. Each beep was meant to be an SOS of some sort from a doctor or nurse wanting us to find a nursing home bed, or to discharge a patient ASAP.

Despite the means to the end, this is all about connection. Connecting with others and feeling that bond to someone else, sometimes anyone else, is what life is all about. We want to reach out and touch someone. We will do it by phone, text, email or some other less personal means if we can't be with them, see them or smell them.

To be able to share an experience with another person is what makes that experience meaningful. Sharing gives us purpose. We seek it out and cherish it.

We may damage a relationship by wanting too much connection, or from seeking love in all the wrong places, but we seek it anyway. For it is that connection that provides the oxygen we need to breathe.

To ensure connection with others at this time of life, you might consider joining or forming gratitude groups, book clubs, journaling groups, co-op gardens, meet-up groups for hiking, coffee, dancing, laughing yoga, or even complaining groups. It is not the topic that is so important—it's the union with others.

Do you have a group of friends who you have known since high school? College? You probably cherish these friends, as they know you on a level others do not, and they still love and accept you. Some of my oldest friends and the ones who know me best are women with different political views and varying religious beliefs. We can agree to disagree and still maintain a very close connection; one that would mean being there for one another in times of need. We can value our core humanity even if our beliefs are dissimilar.

Did you ever live in a commune in the 60's? Would you ever want to live in one now? Many older adults live in communities like Sun City, where the commonalities may be golf, bridge, or simply age.

Other communal living distinctions are typically large gatherings of people sharing a common life. Those gatherings of people may seek out and share a common sense of ideals, outlook on life, sustainable living and or a desire for positive social change. It may be a group of people on the same land, living in different houses, sharing a common garden, but coming together in a shared dining facility where everyone participates in the preparation and serving of the meals. There are communities of artists in New Mexico and Texas that share common values, and in many other states as well.

Living communally may be a way to stay in concert with others our age as we get older. It may be a way to care for each other when living alone or more independently is not a solution. It can be a way to stay connected as we go through the life stages.

VOLUNTEERING/SOCIAL ACTIVISM/GIVING BACK

For some families, volunteering was a value and giving back became ingrained in their family culture. Whether we are still at the height of our careers or winding down our job responsibilities, giving back is a way to stay connected to our lives, others' lives, and our community. Volunteering can prevent the stagnation of which Erikson speaks.

There are many ways to give back. It might mean volunteering at your child's or grandchild's school, participating in a library book drive, tutoring English as a second language for foreign language students, working for a political party to help register to vote, or to help campaign for a candidate whose values you share.

The possibilities available for being socially active are endless; the chances for developing a sense of community spirit and connection are priceless.

Prioritize your top values. Are you living in accordance with those values? This may require deep reflection. A priority is always what you value, yet what you value is not always a priority.

Here are some questions for you to explore through journaling.

ACTION PLAN

1. What were your family values and how were they passed on?

2. What are you grateful for? *Who* are you grateful for? What are some qualities within yourself that you have nurtured and for which you are grateful?

3. What are your self-truths? Explore what is true for you. You will find them in your writing. Write and find the uniqueness that is you.

4. What are your priorities? Do you find that you have more "who" in the priorities rather than things, more than ever before?

5. What is most important to you now in your life? How is it different than in other decades? What makes it so important?

10

JOY TOWARDS THE ANXIOUS WORLD

"When you are joyous, look deep into your heart and you shall find it is only that which has given you sorrow that is giving you joy. When you are sorrowful look again in your heart, and you shall see that in truth you are weeping for that which has been your delight."

Khalil Gibran, *The Prophet*

When we are anxious we may seek relief in pleasure-filled activities with the *hopes* that our worries will somehow fall away and we will be free of our "what if" mindset. If we can find a way to have fun and not think about all those fears and anxieties of the day then we may think, Hallelujah!

In our Western culture, we look for ways to reduce stress, find new coping mechanisms, alleviate anxiety and worry, and find pleasure in our lives. Even though we know that pleasure is fleeting, we still do whatever it takes to seek it, find it, and when it goes away, look for it anew. Yet instead of seeking short-term pleasurable activities to relieve our anxieties, our worries can ultimately be relieved and some may be even eliminated if we explore our grief, sorrow and pain that we are carrying within us to get to the deeper state of joy in our lives.

One way to make the distinction between the meanings of these two often loaded words, pleasure and joy, is to note that pleasure comes from an outside source, tends to be fleeting and depends upon temporal factors like events or other people.

Whereas joy comes from an inside source, inside us.

The word "joy" comes from the Greek root word chara and means "to be exceedingly glad." Chara comes from the Greek word *Charis*, which means "grace." The Greeks believed that Chara is produced by what they call the Charis, or grace, of God, and that joy is not a human-based happiness that comes and goes but that real joy is divine in its origin.

You may believe that your joy comes from God especially if you believe that all things come from God, which would include suffering, pain, sadness, and grief. However, no matter your religious beliefs, if you do the work to relieve your suffering, you can find your joy.

Regardless of the origins of joy, there may be roadblocks between you and your experiencing true joy. By working through your pains, hurts and sufferings, you gain insights into your truths wherein you can lessen your anxieties and worries and open yourself to joy. By examining and exploring your issues, you can remove those obstacles and experience real joy.

Seeking pleasure is a first stage of life pursuit.

In this later stage of life, we search for intrinsic, long-lasting bliss and joy. We want our suffering to be over, yet we know that somehow it is just beginning as we lose people that we love through illness, loss of minds, and death. We wonder, *How can I find joy with all this suffering I must bear?*

Embracing Grief or Embrace the Suck

To be able to embrace grief sounds as though we must hug it, hold it, surrender to it, feel it and experience it to get past it. Who coined that phrase anyway? It sounds like the antithesis of what actually happens when you lose someone.

We want to shed grief, be rid of it, let it go, thump it on its head, push it away, and be done with it. Yet, we need to reframe the suffering as a necessary teacher to finding our joy and bliss. When we feel the pain, only then can we get through it. Feeling our pain deeply allows our healing to include the joy that we so desperately seek, and then we can see the truth in Khalil Gibran's statement.

War veterans of Vietnam, Iraq and Afghanistan use the term "embrace the suck." Benjamin Tupper, a captain in the military who trained Afghan forces against the Taliban, said he remembers first hearing the term "embrace the suck" in 2001, shortly after Afghanistan was invaded by the United States. Tupper wrote in his book *Greetings from Afghanistan,* "The spirits of the American infantrymen were undeterred." He went on to say that "Their Zen-like approach was to 'embrace the suck,' a strategy of treating the hardships as friends, not enemies, and driving on."

In a crude depiction of what the captain meant, he basically is saying that war sucks. His explanation is that a soldier simply sucks it up and moves on. There is no time to pause, grieve, cry, or suffer. The pain is real and it is in the moment. But to take time to feel could mean your death or a buddy's death. Why not befriend the horror instead?

This must be what war is all about. To embrace the suck means to be a smart soldier, one who was well-trained to do his duty to God and his country.

Sounds like a prescription for PTSD, and it is. The paradox is that to be a good soldier means you embrace the horror as a friend so that you can move on. Yet, what happens when all of our veterans return home? That friend can become your worst enemy. That stuffed pain may erupt as early as the plane ride home. Those warriors must now return to a more civilized society in which no one, other than other vets, can truly understand what horrors went down on the battlefields of war.

Our veterans' hospitals are overwhelmed with veterans who have returned from our wars unhealed, or who tried to assimilate back into the real world but could not. Even if you were never in war, but had some other significant trauma in your past like some sort of abuse, emotional, physical or sexual, if you have not healed from it, not allowed yourself to feel it and work through it, now is the time. There is no time like the present one.

In this stage of life, we must remember to embrace the "both *and*" instead of the "either/or," as in embracing the grief and suffering and the eventual joy that will transpire from it. If you are unable to grieve a loss, it may impair your well-being.

So, how do you go from grief, trauma, suffering, pain, and anxiety, to JOY? It may not make sense that you have to feel the pain before you can experience the deep inner joy that is already intrinsic in our soul. If you continue to be haunted by the past, you must uncover the pain, and recover what is already there. Some people say we are born with everything that we need, our soul just gets layers and layers of agonized dust on top of it. We must dust off our souls and uncover the hidden joy.

A recent news report on the network show *60 Minutes* followed a group of war veterans involved in a treatment that had been used with victims of physical and sexual abuse, now being used to treat these vets' Post Traumatic Stress

Disorder over their flashbacks from war and the survivor's guilt that they experience. This program, run by the Veterans Administration Hospital in Little Rock, Arkansas, is about prolonged exposure to the trauma as they verbally recall numerous times a session the events they would rather avoid thinking about.

They also utilize another treatment called cognitive processing therapy where they are encouraged to write about the trauma, to face what they have suppressed since returning from war. When these treatments are used, someone can learn how to manage their anxiety, depression, irritability, hyper-vigilance and other PTSD symptoms.

Instead of pushing the memories away, they can explore and realize the impact and significance these stories have for them.

We may never know the hurt and deep pain each of us experience. It is so individual and so personal, yet so universal. That means that you alone have to know when you are in a place where you can't experience life's joy along with life's pain and find a way to heal.

In Santa Fe, New Mexico, the *New Mexican* newspaper wrote a story about a sixty-year-old retired Marine Corps helicopter mechanic who died from a self-inflicted gunshot wound, alone with his pain from whatever wounds he could not heal. He had been estranged from his family for years, had no close relatives or friends nearby, and was found in his apartment weeks after he took his own life. He also had carefully organized memorabilia from his twenty-year career in the Marine Corps, and a recent clipping of a newspaper story with the headline, "Program ensures that no veteran 'dies alone'."

It was apparent that family estrangements and possible early childhood traumas haunted this man, despite his decorated career. The workers who found him made sure that he would have a military funeral service and organized a burial for him at the National Cemetery.

This speaks to the humanity of strangers who could embrace their grief over a man they did not know, but whose emotional pain they could sense. These workers honored him by finding a way to treat him respectfully after he ended his life. They must have felt a great gratitude for their own lives and great joy that they could make a final tribute for this stranger. If only this veteran had received the help he needed to heal from past wounds, maybe his life would have been different.

HOW INACCURACIES ABOUT ANXIETY CAN PREVENT JOY

One of the top misunderstandings about anxiety is that it needs to be banished from our lives. That until we rid ourselves of it, *forever*, we can't have peace of mind, get on with our present life, our future life, or enjoy the time we have, much less find *joy*, that elusive state of mind that escapes many of us. We think why bother even trying to find it, especially with all this twenty-first century angst.

Yet some anxiety is okay. It is okay because new anxieties will crop up. Your truth can be, "Once I do the work, I can find joy and peace, even if new daily anxieties come up."

The other misconception is that you can outrun your anxiety. Let's say you are in a meeting room filled with co-workers. Your boss informs the group that Tony, another co-worker, is relocating within the same company to another state. Your boss asks if you would each say a few words about Tony and his contributions to the company and to you in your work together.

You begin to think, *Oh no, I have to speak in front of all these people in my own words, right now?* Your anxiety overtakes you and you start to panic for fear of sounding not just nervous but worried about saying something stupid and dumb.

You might think, *I don't even know Tony that well, maybe I can ditch out of here quickly so I won't have to say anything, because I don't know what to say anyway. People will think what I have to say is stupid and dumb and then they will think I am stupid and dumb. He may be leaving but I have to spend the rest of my career with these people. Maybe I can be the first to talk so I won't be nervous and have my voice tremble. Oh God, Betty is going first, she always has to go first. She is such a suck-up.*

So, now you are either second or third, somewhere in between all those other employees, or even last to talk. But you still have the anxiety, because you still have the negative talk that goes with it, the self-talk that is in actuality creating the anxiety you so desperately want to hide and banish forever. You think, *Jeez, I can't even outrun my anxiety right!*

It is true that we can't outrun our anxiety and do it right because it just won't let us. We can't outrun our anxiety because anxiety is not something outside of us that we can escape from by running to another locale. Worry, fret and anxiety are caused by the nasty negative words we are saying to ourselves about ourselves. As long as those unconstructive thoughts are nearby, joy is anywhere but.

Another thought about anxiety is that your religion will free you from anxiety. Some people believe that if you have faith in God then you will never have any fears because you will trust in the Lord thy God, the father Almighty, maker of heaven and earth, and He will take away all those negative worries, fears and what ifs and banish them from one's mind, forever and ever more. I used to think this *should* be true. But when I had faith and still had anxieties, I knew it was just a hopeful thought.

A friend tells me about a man who is devout in his faith. He believes that life after death is in the resurrection which involves God's recreation of the individual with a new body. Any believer who dies will be resurrected in a young body with no physical ailments or disabilities.

She says that her friend is smart, highly educated and teaches on the college level. He can confidently teach classes without self-consciousness as well as speak to his congregation of thousands. But lately he has suffered from severe health anxiety and agoraphobia. He is afraid of taking any medications due to possible side effects and lives in a double bind of abhorring his fears yet being fearful of what to do about them.

Would you question his religious beliefs? Would you wonder if he is not fully invested in them because if he were he would have no fear? What does this say about faith? Could it be that we can have faith and be anxious at the same time?

While it would be wonderful if our faith could take away any of our self-doubts, anxiety, inner turmoil or angst, it is not an either/or situation.

FINDING COMPASSION EVEN WHEN YOU HATE THE MASSES

"Love yourself. Then forget it. Then, love the world." – Mary Oliver, Evidence: Poems

Compassion is an important component to relieving anxiety and finding joy. Without it you may find daily mundane occurrences become full-blown hassles which leave you in a perpetual state of tension and anxiousness.

You may never verbalize that you are not a fan of the masses, those people out there who barge in front of you in their car on the highway, or who sneak in front of you at a checkout line. Those people who take so long to pay their bill at the restaurant, or the ones who are intolerant of the poor, hungry, homeless or mentally ill. You may be secret with these thoughts or you may voice them directly and simply say: "I hate people."

My husband and I were newcomers to our recent hometown by a few months when we decided to try out a new restaurant for breakfast. The two- and four-tops were taken on this busy Sunday morning so we chose to sit at the only free seats at the large rectangular table in the center of the room. We sat down next to a couple who appeared to be close to our ages that were holding hands deep in quiet conversation.

"Are these seats reserved for anyone?" my husband and I asked in tandem.

"Oh no," the attractive, silver-haired lady replied. "Go ahead."

Being new in town and having heard that people easily strike up a conversation with strangers here in restaurants, we tried it out for ourselves.

"Have you all been here before?" I asked. It was a new restaurant and the likelihood was slim, yet I was breaking into their conversation with the most mundane line I could. It wasn't long before my husband and this woman, the man's wife, began talking politics. I struck up a conversation with the jocular husband, an intelligent, joke-cracking guy.

Shortly after we began to acquaint ourselves with our new friends, I heard this silver-haired woman respond excitedly, "Me too!" I looked over at my husband who laughingly remade his provocative comment.

"I hate people," he told me when I requested a second verbalization of what he had just said.

This wasn't the first time I had heard him say this in mixed company. The first time was way harder for me to digest. We were at a party at a fine restaurant for the staff at St. Edward's University's Master of Counseling program, for which I was an adjunct professor. The invitation was for a Christmas get-together to celebrate the season and to thank all of the professors and staff of this program. Talking with a colleague, we shared pleasantries and gratitude for the invitation to this glorious Christmas affair.

I noticed that my colleague's wife was entranced with my husband's comments about the wonderful quail appetizers that were part of the spread of hors d'oeuvres at the buffet. A new tray of quail had just been brought in and several men stalked the tray, my husband included. My anxiety kept me from being fully engrossed in the conversation. I was keeping an eye out for the Dean of Students, whom I wanted to thank for having us.

From the quail to the safety of our back corner of the room I heard my colleague's wife laugh and say, "I hate people too."

I looked over at my now suspect husband and said, "What did you just say?"

"I told her I don't like these kinds of events and when she asked why I told her 'Because did you see how that guy got in front of me to grab as many quail as he could? I hate people.'"

My only bag of tricks in that moment for anxiety was to quietly mouth the mantra "Ooommmm."

Those masses are easy for some people to hate. They are the unknowns, the un-persons, the others, the ones who take up space on our planet and who are inconsiderate and unkind. They never think of us first, only of themselves.

One definition of compassion is "sympathetic pity and concern for the sufferings or misfortunes of others." Yet, that explanation conjures up a victim mentality in which someone else has done something to cause where they are in their life. Maybe another way to look at compassion is to have passion for or an understanding of another's pain, foibles, travails, and even suffering, and to see them like us.

If you hate the masses, you may not have much compassion for yourself. If you did, you would see that we are all alike even with our dissimilarities. To dislike anyone else is to not have compassion for yourself. You may believe all those nasty things you think about yourself which can translate to nasty thoughts about others.

A laundry list of psychological factors can be the culprit for hating the masses. A lack of nurturing parents, or neglect in our childhood can increase the likelihood that we won't have compassion for ourselves. Past traumas from which we have not healed could be a dynamic. A belief we are not making a difference in the world could be a cause.

Despite the possible causes, it may be difficult to appreciate the beauty in others when it is hard to see it within yourself. Anxiety can reign when we let those others get the best of us.

VULNERABLE IS AS VULNERABLE DOES

"Owning our story can be hard but not nearly as difficult as spending our lives running from it. Embracing our vulnerabilities is risky but not nearly as dangerous as giving up on love and belonging and joy—the experiences that make us the most vulnerable. Only when we are brave enough to explore the darkness will we discover the infinite power of our light."— Brené Brown

The definitions of vulnerability are not cherished ones. The two Webster definitions are: capable of being physically or emotionally wounded, or open to attack or damage, as in "He opened himself up emotionally and was vulnerable to criticism."

We need to be cautious in situations of possible physical attack. You wouldn't go into a bullring without training, yet the mere act of stepping into one with a live bull puts you in a vulnerable position. You may get hurt, gored, or be killed. Yet, bullfighters do this by choice. Extreme skiers, rock- and ice climbers put themselves in risky and dangerous locations and positions for the sheer thrill of it.

But being emotionally vulnerable is often seen as being weak, losing power, opening oneself up to be taken advantage of by another person. So, instead of feeling or expressing any emotional pain, we may get on the defensive, or close down our emotions. Or we may get on the offensive and act aggressively to feel strong and powerful to embolden ourselves.

Dr. Brené Brown found evidence in her research and studies on vulnerability that if you deaden or prevent vulnerability, you are also numbing any joy and happiness. Embracing your vulnerability can help you discover that compassion within, for yourself and for others. Allowing yourself to be open to hurt or emotional pain will be healing and transforming despite how fearful you may be to try it. It is listening to your heart and soul and heeding the sounds.

Being vulnerable can allow you to laugh and cry at the same time. Maybe you have experienced that phenomenon before. What a gift to open yourself to the moment and feel whatever it was that you were feeling or experiencing like laughing through your tears. Like nervousness and excitement, laughter and tears are similar physiologically.

I remember sitting with my close friend, Debbie, and her mother in the limousine at the head of a long line of cars, traveling to the funeral services for Debbie's father Norm. Debbie, who was known for her funny antics, sat in the back seat along with her mother and me. Debbie fiddled with her purse, pulled out her compact and wiped the mirror with her finger to clear the powder residues. She held it to the side and moved it around until she got the best vantage point she could.

"What are you doing?" I asked.

"I'm checking to see how long the procession is and how many cars are behind us," she chuckled. We both laughed through our tears.

What a gift to be able to laugh at that moment despite the heavy loss that we all felt. When you experience the in-the-moment pleasure that comes from a momentary lift of a heavy burden of loss, you let go of any guilt that you would ordinarily feel, because you aren't wondering whether you should or should not have laughed during that tense moment. You are being vulnerable to the moment, in that delightful place of being real, open and honest with yourself.

"Perhaps I know best why it is man alone who laughs; he alone suffers so deeply that he had to invent laughter." – Friedrich Nietzsche

This quote reminds me of that saying about courage that can be so helpful to repeat when you might be feeling weak or fearful; feel the fear and do it anyway. The "it" being whatever action you are afraid of taking. You don't have to be fearful of any negative emotions. They are part of you and part of the process of healing.

By acknowledging any suffering from our past traumas and allowing ourselves to be vulnerable by feeling any emotional pain, we can see from where we have come, and be grateful for where we are now. This is how we will come to experience joy towards ourselves and others. Now.

ACTION PLAN

1. What event in your life has caused you the most suffering and pain? What effects has it had on your life? How do you feel about it today?

2. How have you been open and vulnerable in your life? How has it made a difference? What is the worst that could happen if you were vulnerable?

3. Did you ever experience joy in the first half of life? Is it different from this second half? How does joy manifest itself now in your life?

4. Can you identify with people who say, "I hate people," or "I hate the masses?" What makes that true, or false, for you?

5. Have you had a loss that you have not grieved? Can you write about it now?

11

LET IT BE

"Whisper words of wisdom, let it be"

The Beatles

"We do not receive wisdom; we must discover it for ourselves after a journey through the wilderness, which no one else can make for us, which no one can spare us, for our wisdom is the point of view from which we come at last to regard the world."

Marcel Proust

You now know that if you deal with the issues of your past, you can rid yourself of the anxieties of your history. You know that by living in the moment, you can rid yourself of the anxieties of the future. If you have no unwarranted anxiety over the past or the future, you are freed up to focus and deal with any concerns of the moment, which are the only legitimate concerns. While it may sound like a daunting task to be able to transform our worries to wonder, it can be as simple as utilizing some of the techniques listed in this guide.

To achieve transformation does not necessarily require long-term therapy. If you have more complicated issues which require a deeper, longer period of work to help you grieve, get through some suffering or past issues, then you may want to visit with a professional to process your feelings and thoughts in a safe setting.

At this time of life, we can let go of some of our early worries and find ways to have serenity with the realities of the now. We may still be afraid of the unknown, yet we can be at peace with that and find joy in life even with that anxiety. We don't need all the explanations for the questions about which we wonder. We can find our individual truths and personal answers that can allow us to accept ourselves and find peace of mind.

You can say your words of wisdom, and then let it be.

If you are letting your anxieties make your choices for you because you are afraid of taking a risk beyond your usual and customary actions, take that first step out of the bind of anxiety and into the courage of your life. The courage that says, "This may scare the crap out of me, but I am going to do it anyway. I do not want to live in fear at this time in my life. I choose courage and faith that I can do this."

TAKE ACTION BY USING ONE OR MORE ACTIVITIES ON THIS LIST:

1. Meditating

2. Journaling

3. Tapping

4. Setting aside worry time

5. Prayer—it can be a way to verbalize your fears and then let them go. You can use the Serenity Prayer, or your own words.

6. Use the Cognitive cycle to identify your negative thoughts, challenge them, and then reframe them to more realistic ones.

7. Acknowledge and embrace any anxiety you feel in your body: breathe deeply, take a walk, run in place for five minutes, attend a Yoga class, a dance class, water aerobics, laugh, listen to music and sing along, visit a naturopath or chiropractor on a regular basis to stay healthy, acupuncture for any physical pain.

Lay down the regrets of your past and let go of any shame that still haunts you. Transform any worries to wonder by finding awe in that which you do not understand. When you can be grateful for what you *have,* you will discover the joy that is all around you, even with the anxieties of the present.

That is piece of mind and the joy of anxiety.

Go for it. Whatever "it" is.

The. Future. Is. Now.

APPENDIX

TAPPING/EMOTIONAL FREEDOM TECHNIQUE

Nick Ortner is the creator of the *Tapping Solution: A Revolutionary System for Stress-Free Living*. In his book, he offers ways to rid you of unwanted anxieties and fears that you may have had for years, or something that you may have just discovered that is causing you distress and pain.

I want to introduce you to Tapping with the following model. You can use this technique for any worry or fear, phobia, grief, depressed mood, past or present trauma, obsessive thoughts, compulsive behaviors and even physical pain, which can often be related to our mental state of being. All you have to do is change the words. You want to start with the actual thoughts you are saying to yourself about yourself, as those are real beliefs that you want to address.

To start, give your issue a number 0-10, with 10 being the most intense and 0 or 1 being no distress at all. The higher the intensity of the feelings or thoughts, the greater the chance that you will be in a state to lessen that anxiety. Then create your setup statement, or words to describe what you are thinking (see below for an example), and start tapping with two to three fingers of one hand on the parts of the body below. When you start with the Karate Chop, you tap on the soft part of the opposite hand below the pinkie with a perpendicular chop of that hand. This particular setup is for those with fear of public speaking. It is important to include in each segment the following words, as in the first two examples, *I completely and deeply accept myself.*

Karate Chop: Even though I'm stressed about what they'll think of me, I completely and deeply accept myself.

Eyebrow: Even though it makes me nervous to speak in front of other people, *I completely and deeply accept myself.*
Side of the eye: Freaks me out.
Under eye: Too many people.
Under nose: Don't like all the attention.
Chin: So many people watching.
Collarbone: Too many people.
Under arm: Too much attention.
Top of head: Stresses me out.

Keep tapping until you feel relief, and then check in with yourself. You'll want to continue tapping until your anxiety is a 3 or lower. At that point, you're ready to tap in some positive emotion, which is what we'll do now. You don't need a setup statement for this.

Eyebrow: I choose to trust that they'll love my talk!
Side of the eye: So many people coming to hear what I have to say.
Under eye: Lots of people interested in my topic.
Under nose: I can definitely keep people engaged in what I'm saying.

Chin: So much great energy!

Collarbone: Exciting to share my message with all these people.

Under arm: I am really well prepared.

Top of head: This is going to be great!

Keep tapping like this until you're feeling grounded in that positive emotion, and as always, use your own words when you're tapping. The statements above are just examples.

You can find more information at Nick Ortner's website. You can view his videos on You Tube of how to go through this model:www.thetappingsolution.com.

This style of Tapping is a bit different from Dr. Roger Callahan's formulas and algorithms in his book, *Tapping the Healer Within.* I have used them both with great success. You can try each of them and see what might work best for you.

RESOURCES

Adams, K. (1990). *Journal to the Self: Twenty-Two Paths to Personal Growth.* New York: Warner Books.

Bourne, E. (2010). *The Anxiety and Phobia Workbook.* Oakland: New Harbinger Publications.

Callahan, Roger J. (2001). *Tapping the Healer Within: Using Thought Field Therapy to Instantly Conquer Your Fears, Anxieties and Emotional Distress.* New York: McGraw-Hill.

Erikson, Erik H., Erikson, Joan M., Kivnick Helen Q. (1986). *Vital Involvement in Old Age.* New York: W.W. Norton & Company, Inc.

Moore, Thomas (1992). *Care of the Soul: A Guide for Cultivating Depth and Sacredness in Everyday Life.* New York: Harper Collins.

Ortner, Nick (2013). *The Tapping Solution: A Revolutionary System for Stress-Free Living.* New York: Hay House, Inc.

Rohr, Richard (2011). *Falling Upward: A Spirituality for the Two Halves of Life.* San Francisco: Jossey-Bass.

Wilson, Reid R. (1996). *Don't Panic: Taking Control of Anxiety Attacks.* New York: Harper Collins.

ACKNOWLEDGMENTS

Gratitude and love to my husband Don, the real writer in the family, who despite his ADD and some compulsive traits which he has come to accept as anxieties, helped me with my words. When he tells me how I have helped him it makes all of my years of anxiety worth it.

Thank you to: Patti Lemons LCSW, a colleague in Austin for recommending Roger Callahan's book on Tapping when I looked for something more for a client with obsessive compulsive behaviors; Roger Callahan, who discovered this wonderful technique which has helped so many with anxiety; Nick Ortner for following in his footsteps and helping masses of people heal their physical and emotional pain; Marilyn Nichols, who taught us the technique that relieved my fears with Nada.

Thank you to Kris Bakula, my college roommate who gave me fodder for a story; Willis Weigand, for your story about your first-year college students and for getting how perfectionism can dampen real creativity, and for heading it off at the pass.

Thanks to Bill O'Hanlon for your Book Writing and Publishing Course, your expert guidance, and supportive feedback.

Thank you to Carolyn Scarborough, my writing coach for *The Joy of Nada,* who allowed me to share our spiritual story; my friend Toni Sams, whose career jaunts I mention; my friend Geena Thomas for her lovely way of writing and her exclamation I used; my colleague Reid Minot, who kindly provided fodder for a story; my friend Holly Prescott, who, along with Kelly White, got me back on track about my title; Sara McMillan, my friend and colleague for giving me the word that perfected my title, and to Jill Buskirk Johns for her encouragement to write a second book.

Gratitude for the sweet serendipity that occurred when we met our new friends Robin and Peter at a restaurant and with whom we shared a synchronistic experience when Robin later told me she too had memorized the back of a Crest toothpaste tube as a child!

My love and gratitude to my family, who understand how anxiety and joy could coexist in our childhood household.

Special thanks to my wise therapist, mentor and spiritual advisor Sam Cangelosi, LCSW, who never labeled me with any anxiety disorder but who instead helped me with whatever concerns I had.

Gratitude to Justine Tal Goldberg at WriteByNight who edited my manuscript and who always answers any questions with patience and compassion.

Gratitude for our new friends, Thaddeus and Teresa Kostrubala, authors of *The Joy of Running* and *The Joy of Running 2*. If meeting them and finding out they wrote these two special and joyful books wasn't synchronistic enough, they also introduced me to Dominick Bosco, author of *Bedlam, A Year In The Life Of A Mental Hospital*. Dominick created the print version of *The Joy of Anxiety*. Thank you, Dominick, for all your assistance in getting this ready for print, and for the integrity you put into your awesome work.

And thank you to all my clients who have been helped by some of these techniques, and whose sessions have produced in-the-moment healing wisdom for us all.

ABOUT THE AUTHOR

Sue Genaro Legacy is a Licensed Clinical Social Worker and Psychotherapist in private practice who specializes in helping anyone in the second stage of life discover more meaning and purpose. She has been an Adjunct Professor in the Master of Counseling program at St. Edward's University. Her first book, *The Joy of Nada: A Memoir of Self Discovery* was published in August of 2013. Her podcast, The Joy of Anxiety, is available on iTunes and Stitcher radio. Sue currently lives in Santa Fe, New Mexico with her husband and two Chihuahua mix dogs, Nada and Todo.

Sue Legacy offers workshops, and coaching to individuals and groups. Contact her at Email: info@thejoyofanxiety.com.

Special Offer

I am interested in your feedback. Please email me with what was helpful to you, and I will send you a free copy of *How Being Imperfect Is The Perfect Way To Be.*

Best to you in your endeavors!

info@thejoyofanxiety.com

www.thejoyofanxiety.com

www.suelegacy.com

Digital Presence

Scan this QR code with your smartphone to visit my
website:
www.suelegacy.com

And visit me on these social media links, which you can
access through my website or with these QR codes:

Facebook:

Twitter

Podcasts/iTunes

Linked In

82619556R00111

Made in the USA
Middletown, DE
04 August 2018